WHAT PEOPLE ARE SAYING ABOUT

THE PRINCE AND THE WOLF

Too often debates are sterile. Each participant lines up behind the other, each with their own point of view. All is on show but nothing much happens. This debate is different. Something happened.
Nigel Thrift, Vice-Chancellor of the University of Warwick
Author of *Non-representational Theory: Space, Politics, Affect* (2008), *Knowing Capitalism* (2005), and *Spatial Formations* (1996)

This is an especially welcome book. It is rare that one has the opportunity to be a near eye witness to a constructive and intellectually generous exchange of provocative ideas-in-the-making. Graham Harman, Bruno Latour and the assembled audience put on a great show. The exchange is fresh, laced with good humor, and informative. There is much to be learned here about empirical metaphysics—and collegiality.
Michael Flower, Portland State University

Many crucial things get exposed and made explicit here. A key access point to the Latourian moment.
Fabian Muniesa, École des Mines de Paris

The Prince and the Wolf

Latour and Harman at the LSE

The Prince and the Wolf

Latour and Harman at the LSE

Bruno Latour, Graham Harman
and Peter Erdélyi

Winchester, UK
Washington, USA

First published by Zero Books, 2011
Zero Books is an imprint of John Hunt Publishing Ltd., Laurel House, Station Approach,
Alresford, Hants, SO24 9JH, UK
office1@o-books.net
www.o-books.com

For distributor details and how to order please visit the 'Ordering' section on our website.

Text copyright: Bruno Latour, Graham Harman, and Peter Erdélyi 2010

ISBN: 978 1 84694 422 2

A CIP catalogue record for this book is available from the British Library.

Design: Stuart Davies

Printed in the UK by CPI Antony Rowe
Printed in the USA by Offset Paperback Mfrs, Inc

We operate a distinctive and ethical publishing philosophy in all
areas of our business, from our global network of authors to
production and worldwide distribution.

CONTENTS

Acknowledgement

We would like to thank the Information Systems and Innovation Group at the London School of Economics and Political Science for their generous support in hosting the symposium "The Harman Review: Bruno Latour's Empirical Metaphysics" and producing this transcript.

Foreword

The Prince and the Wolf is a modern-day fairy tale in which the
protagonists, instead of resorting to physical violence, decide to
settle their differences in a debate on metaphysics. The reasons for
the allegory will soon become clear. This volume contains the
lightly edited transcript of "The Harman Review: Bruno Latour's
Empirical Metaphysics," a symposium held at the London School
of Economics and Political Science (LSE) on February 5, 2008. The
event was a debate staged between Bruno Latour, the prominent
French sociologist, anthropologist, and philosopher of science, an
early developer of actor-network theory (ANT), and Graham
Harman, the Cairo-based American philosopher known for his
post-Heideggerian object-oriented philosophy. Harman's recently
completed manuscript about Latour's contribution to
philosophy—since then published as *Prince of Networks: Bruno
Latour and Metaphysics*—was the main subject of the discussion.[1]
The 'Prince,' remaining true to his fabled sense of humor,
compared the dogged determination of professional philosophers
like Harman who have been pursuing him over the years to that of
a pack of wolves. *The Prince and the Wolf* is the story of what
happens when the wolf catches up with the prince but, through a
strange turn of events, they both find themselves transported to a
laboratory, where they have to contend with each other according
to the rules put in place by the onlooking scientists and their
apprentices. The latter were a diverse, multidisciplinary crowd of
academics and PhD students who gathered to assess the merits of
both Latour's philosophy and Harman's manuscript.

Two sets of questions dominated the proceedings. The first set
concerned the fundamental question *"What is?"*, whether one calls
things that exist beings, actors, or objects. Harman's term *object*
emerged as the favored designator at the event, so I will stick with
it. What is the nature of objects? How do objects emerge? How do

1

objects interact? What is the nature of causality? The second set of questions concentrated on the philosophical practice of *defining what is*, or in other words, metaphysics. What is the purpose of metaphysics? How to conduct metaphysics? What is the relationship between metaphysics and science?

This symposium was an unusual occasion on a number of counts. It is a rare privilege in the best of times to gain access to a contemporary philosopher's work-in-progress manuscript and to have him at hand to discuss it with his readers. It must be an even rarer occurrence also to have the subject of his monograph present and ready to respond. As the eighty or so "[LAUGHTER]" notations in the transcript testify, for a metaphysics conference it was a highly entertaining affair. Those working in philosophy departments may also wonder why the work of a sociologist and anthropologist was being discussed in terms of first philosophy. If one further considers that this proto-philosophical debate was hosted by the Information Systems and Innovation Group (ISIG) in the LSE's Department of Management, the bewilderment must be complete.

Yet there were some very good reasons for this event to unfold the way it did, where it did. Graham Harman's claim is indeed that Bruno Latour the social scientist has made some crucial contributions to philosophy, to which professional philosophers should pay heed. In his words, "When the centaur of classical metaphysics is mated with the cheetah of actor-network theory, their offspring is not some hellish monstrosity, but a thoroughbred colt able to carry us for half a century and more."[2] His sentence conjures up the image of a peculiar laboratory where such cross-breeding of mythological creatures and wild animals can take place. It is however an eminently suitable metaphor for describing this event. The symposium *was* a temporary laboratory for a social science experiment, to test Harman's claims about Latour's metaphysics and Latour's claims about his own work, by subjecting both to an experimental protocol. The task of the audience and the panel —the latter

2

composed of Lucas Introna and Noortje Marres— was to study the sparks that erupted from the collision of the two actors, or in Harman's terminology, of the two objects.

It may strike some readers as odd to hear this encounter of two authors, two flesh-and-blood human beings, described as the clashing of two objects in a laboratory. However, it was precisely the question of what an object as such *is* (whether human or nonhuman) that constituted the central metaphysical controversy of the event. The answers propagated were anything but ordinary. In fact, there was a multitude of objects coming together and interacting at the symposium. Besides the corporeal presence of Harman and Latour, the written corpus of each author and a host of others from the history of philosophy and science were summoned to collide, to shape the arguments of one or the other, including Latour's claim that the *body corporate* (the corporation as an organization) would be an ideal metaphor and case study material for metaphysics.

But who would be interested in such an experiment and why? First and foremost, social science PhD students, in this particular case the PhD students in information systems (IS) who organized this event, and for whom actor-network theory in general and Latour's work in particular has been a major source of inspiration and fascination but also puzzlement for some time. PhD stands for Doctor of Philosophy, after the Latin *philosophiæ doctor*, which at least in the social sciences carries the obligation to examine and declare one's philosophical position in relation to the bit of reality one proposes to study, usually in a chapter on methodology or research philosophy. For IS students, there is the added complication to have to account not only for social phenomena (often defined in terms of groups of humans) but also for technological artifacts. "How do you conceptualize the information and communication technology (ICT) artifact?" is one dreaded but inevitable question that every IS PhD student faces at some point in his or her career.

As Leslie Willcocks and Edgar Whitley point out in a recent article, despite this imperative to consider the philosophical aspects of technology for social research,

> IS, of all subject areas, has no real long-standing philosophical depth or roots in a philosophy of information or of technology. (...) On technology, there is much striving at the margins to utilize, for example, Heidegger, actor-network theory, Habermas, critical realism, various social theories, and philosophies of science. But, otherwise, major philosophical and ethical questions on technology receive all too little in-depth treatment.[3]

It was this need for a philosophical understanding of both technology and social research that drove a small group of PhD students in the LSE's Information Systems department[4] in November 2006 to set up a reading group named ANTHEM (acronym for Actor-Network Theory – Heidegger Meeting), dedicated to the parallel study of the works of Bruno Latour and Martin Heidegger; a line of inquiry that culminated in the organizing of the Harman Review.

There were a number of reasons for this dual focus and juxtaposition. The initial two founders of the group, Aleksi Aaltonen and I, both came with prior knowledge of one of the thinkers and were intensely interested to find out more about the other. At the same time, we were intrigued by the commonalities but also the disagreements between Heidegger and Latour, especially when it came to conceptualizing technological artifacts. Heidegger's essay, "The Question Concerning Technology"[5] has long been a central point of reference for students of technology, as a rare statement by a major philosopher about the nature of technology and its relationship to the pressing questions of the day. Bruno Latour's case studies and philosophical essays also took the question of technology seriously, as if to continue Heidegger's investigation. And yet, he had come to diametrically opposed conclusions about the nature of techno-logical artifacts. At one point Latour even goes as far as to say that "I always find it baffling that people would take Heidegger's 'philosophy of technology' seriously," although in the same breath he praises him for sending "the inquiry in the right direction— that any artifact is a form of assembling, of gathering, of 'thinging' entities together and that it is absurd to forget the mortals and the gods when describing a piece of hardware, even the most hyper-modern ones."[6] This was a relationship too intriguing to ignore.

However, we in the ANTHEM group were by far not the first ones to notice that there was something interesting going on between Heidegger and Latour. There was already a reasonably long history of examining this relationship in the Information Systems Department at the LSE, where a number of researchers had a longstanding interest in Heidegger. Claudio Ciborra (with Ole Hanseth) and Edgar Whitley discussed and deployed Heidegger and actor-network theory side-by-side as early as 1998, which were quite possibly among the very first attempts to do so in print.[7] Lucas Introna, who later moved to Lancaster University, similarly has made a number of important contributions to the ANT-Heidegger nexus.[8] If we add to this the fact that Bruno Latour was a visiting professor in this department between 1999 and 2001, the mystery of why and how the LSE's Information Systems and Innovation Group had emerged as the host for this metaphysical discussion becomes a lot less puzzling. It was at the LSE that Latour conducted the hilarious and by now legendary "(Somewhat) Socratic Dialogue"[9] with an IS PhD student about actor-network theory, which became the perfect antidote to the gloomy vision of Heidegger's "The Question Concerning Technology."

Since 1998 there were several other attempts even outside of the LSE at comparing and contrasting —or even combining— Heidegger and Latour, or phenomenology and actor-network theory.[10] No one, however, has been as persistent and as incisive in pursuing the assessment of Bruno Latour's philosophical adventures from a Heideggerian perspective as Graham Harman. In his 2009 book *Prince of Networks*, Harman not only develops the most thorough evaluation of Latour's empirical metaphysics to date, he also proposes a way to fuse the achievements of both Heidegger and Latour for the furthering of philosophy. Actually, as Harman revealed at the event, his history of engagement with Latour's work also stretches back to 1998: the year in which he "became a Latourian." His 1999 paper "Bruno Latour, King of Networks," presented at the Department of Philosophy at DePaul University, can be seen in retrospect as the seed that grew into the *Prince of Networks* over the ensuing decade.[11] The wolf has been pursuing the prince for a long time indeed.

A central tenet of actor-network theory, adopted from ethnomethodology, is the need to respect the metaphysics of the actors one is studying— and there was a lot of it to respect at this workshop. To be faithful to the two protagonists of our fairy tale (and trust me, it was a dream come true for the PhD students who organized it), it would be prudent to describe the event in their own terms. Both speakers agreed on the principle of generalized symmetry, not to grant ontological privileges to one class of objects over others prior to an inquiry, regardless of their shape, size, or materiality, whether they are human or nonhuman. They also agreed that specific objects need to be taken seriously in metaphysics. An object-oriented description of our event that traces the actions and births of specific artifacts would therefore be in order.

Some of these artifacts could be rather complex, too. Bruno Latour characterized the symposium as one particular "experimental apparatus," namely the ANTHEM apparatus. In this laboratory setting, where ANT and Heidegger are laid side-by-side so that the testing of Latour's contribution to philosophy can be undertaken, some of the experimental subject's attributes would be revealed, but not others. It would be fitting therefore to describe, in object-oriented terms, how this experiment came to be, how the laboratory was set up —how the prince and the wolf got to be ensnared in it— but also to lay bare the experimental protocol which was used to conduct the experiment and which has made certain qualities visible, at the expense of others. Then the readers of the transcript might be in a better position to judge for themselves the outcomes of this experiment.

As suggested earlier, there were two initial and very hazy objects that set off the series of events leading to the symposium. The first one was the rather general object of technology (as IS students, our prime object of study), which was further entangled in other complicated and specific objects such as information systems and organizations. The second object, just as vague and only present as an objective, was the future artifact of the doctoral thesis itself. By getting caught in the gravitational fields of both, we were gradually pulled towards the Heidegger-Latour axis of the debate on the nature of objects and technological artifacts. In Latour's texts we kept running into references to the books of a certain Graham Harman, who tended to pop up whenever key Heideggerian concepts such as 'the thing as gathering' (*Das Ding*) or 'the fourfold' (*Das Geviert*) were mentioned.[12] This had compelled us to read the two books by Harman that were then in print, *Tool-Being* and *Guerrilla Metaphysics*, which offered a refreshingly new interpretation of Heidegger and phenomenology that also pointed towards Latour as someone with very interesting answers to many of Heidegger's questions.

When we heard that in April 2007 Harman was going to give a talk on "Networks and Assemblages: The Rebirth of Things in Latour and DeLanda" at Goldsmiths College in London, the ANTHEM posse, consisting of stalwarts Ofer Engel, Wifak Houij Gueddana and myself, descended on Greenwich. We weren't disappointed. Harman exceeded our expectations by delivering a fascinating talk and agreeing with my comment that there was something about the Heidegger-Latour relation. While we couldn't stay to chat to him after the event, he happily gave us the only printed copy of his talk, which was scanned and shared between us the same day. Two weeks later Harman's *Heidegger Explained* hit the bookshops, which confirmed to us once more that in the person of Harman we had stumbled upon a most interesting link between Heidegger and Latour. As some of us were also planning to take on the organizing of the student-run Information Systems Research Forum (ISRF) in the department, we started discussing the possibility of inviting Harman to speak to us on the issue of Heidegger and Latour in the coming term.

It was therefore a very pleasant surprise when one day in early August 2007 I found an email from Graham Harman in my mailbox. It turned out that he had joined our ANTHEM Google Group mailing list, having been invited by Ofer, who in turn found him on the social networking site Facebook (which incidentally was Ofer's research interest). Soon enough we were engaged in a flurry of online exchanges about all things Heidegger and Latour. We couldn't believe our luck when we found out that Harman was just about to finish his manuscript on Latour's philosophy, which he was ready to share with us electronically. As some of us were gearing up to our Master of Philosophy upgrade events, busy writing our PhD proposals, the manuscript clarifying Latour's philosophy was a gift from heaven, arriving just at the right time.

Before long, Harman had accepted our invitation to take part in two events at the LSE: to give a talk "On Actors, Networks, and Plasma: Heidegger vs. Latour vs. Heidegger"[13] at the Information Systems Research Forum on November 29, 2007, and then to return on February 5, 2008 for a workshop we dubbed his "mini-Cerisy." The idea for the latter was to follow the example of Bruno Latour's ingenious conference at Cerisy-La-Salle in France in June 2007, where he gathered his friends (including Harman) to receive their feedback about his latest manuscript on "the modes of existence."[14] We thought that we could similarly distribute Harman's *Prince of Networks* manuscript among a select group of people and organize a workshop on a smaller scale, where it could be constructively reviewed.

However, on October 18, 2007 another unexpected email arrived via the ANTHEM Google Group, posted by one of our members, with the subject line: "Latour in London tomorrow." As we had just begun discussing his *Reassembling the Social* book in our reading group that week, we were all keen to take this opportunity to meet the man himself. Latour spoke at the Serpentine Gallery in Hyde Park.[15] He graciously chatted with our ANTHEM contingent of four both before and after the event, and autographed the Latour volumes each of us was clutching. He reminisced about his time at the LSE, asked us to pass on his warm regards to the people he still knew there, and generally seemed very amused about the existence of a Heidegger-Latour reading group. When it was time to say our goodbyes, he said (I'm quoting freely): "Wait a second. I'll be coming to the LSE to give a lecture sometime next year," at which point he reached into his pocket and took out his Palm handheld, to check the exact date. Being a proud owner of a Palm TX, I also took out mine. And this was the moment when not only the two Palm Pilots but also the stars became aligned, as we established that Bruno Latour and Graham Harman would both be at the LSE on February 4-5, 2008.

In *Reassembling the Social*, in sharp contrast to Heidegger's stark opposition between being and the nothing,[16] Latour suggests that "...there might exist many metaphysical shades between full causality and sheer inexistence"[17]; this moment then was definitely one of the many mini-births of the Harman Review. Considering that a leading scholar of science and technology and PhD students of information systems were involved, it seemed most fitting that technological artifacts such as the Google Group, Facebook, PDF copies of Harman's manuscript, the Palm handhelds and the ANTHEM blog all played such indispensible part in the midwifery that brought this symposium to life. However, the task of organizing the event had only just begun, and we faced a number of challenges. In the months that followed (and there weren't that many, with the Christmas break in the middle), we had to painstakingly enroll, one by one, all the relevant stakeholders needed to make this thing work.

When I refer to our little colloquium as 'this thing,' it's not an attempt on my part to sound colloquial but to weave in the Heideggerian notion of the thing as gathering (*Das Ding*), which also appears to be Latour's favorite Heideggerian concept, though with some modifications. Always the great etymologist, Heidegger made the following discovery ('recovery' would be a better word) for philosophy: "the Old High German word *thing* means a gathering, and specifically a gathering to deliberate on a matter under discussion, a contested matter."[18] In *Making Things Public*, Bruno Latour makes the link even more explicit between the *thing* as an object and the *thing* as a parliament (the words for parliament and thing are still almost identical in some Nordic countries).[19] The thing that assembles, the thing that is an assembly, is the perfect metaphor for Latour to emphasize the relational, heterogeneous, contested and constructed character of things, what he calls "matters of concern." It would be most appropriate then to describe the assembling of our particular gathering as a thing, an assembly which concerned itself with the contested matter of metaphysics.

The building of our thing, our temporary laboratory, consisted of gathering all the necessary elements to construct the site (the experimental setup) and develop the program (the experimental protocol), two tasks that in practice were indistinguishable. First we formed the symposium organising committee, made up of Aleksi, Ofer, Wifak, and I, all doctoral students, later joined by Maha Shaikh, a Research Officer at ISIG. Then we needed to get the Information Systems and Innovation Group on board, as without their material, moral, and intellectual support the event would have remained a pipe dream. We were fortunate to find a pillar of support in Edgar Whitley, Reader in Information Systems, who proved to be instrumental in helping out both with advice on the format and with technical details such as the booking of the room. Whitley emerged as the ideal impartial chair for the event, given his parallel interests in Heidegger and ANT, which go back to the time of Latour's stay in the department. Professor Leslie Willcocks, the head of ISIG, was also an enthusiastic and generous supporter of the symposium from the start, providing much needed institutional and financial support and a warm welcome to the participants on the day.

Another important milestone was the formal acceptance of the two protagonists to take part, which, as I pointed out earlier, was facilitated by the movement of the stars. Besides our mini-Cerisy, Graham Harman planned to be in England in February 2008 anyway thanks to an impressive series of talks he had been invited to give, crisscrossing the country from south to north and east to west, from Bournemouth to Lancaster, from Bristol to Milton Keynes.[20] Bruno Latour was coming to London to deliver a high-profile lecture at the LSE on February 4, 2008, as part of the Franco-British Europe Dialogues sponsored by the LSE European Institute, Sciences Po and the French Embassy.[21] It was therefore relatively straightforward to settle on the February 5 date, especially since Harman's manuscript had already done the work of enrolling Bruno Latour.

Being the PhD students that we were, hungry for some answers, from the outset we were interested in making the event as interactive and constructive as possible. While at the time we hadn't thought of it as an experiment (not until Bruno Latour uttered the word on the very day), we did want the event to produce some answers for everyone involved: for both of our speakers working on their respective manuscripts, for the audience with their diverse interests, and of course for our own projects. The idea of getting other scholars of Heidegger and/or ANT to engage with our speakers therefore came up early on. It went through a number of iterations, until finally we settled on the idea of having a panel of experts. We were extremely fortunate to be able to convince Lucas

Introna and Noortje Marres to become our panelists, as they fit the bill perfectly thanks to their research interests and expertise as well as their historical links to the LSE's Information Systems department and the speakers themselves.

Professor Lucas Introna, the head of the Department of Organisation, Work and Technology at Lancaster University Management School, had been working at the LSE at the time of Latour's visiting professorship. With his long-standing research interests in phenomenology, Heidegger, the philosophy of technology and also the work of Latour, he was ideally suited to take on the role of the resident Heideggerian panelist. Noortje Marres, at the time a Marie Curie Research Fellow in the Department of Sociology at Goldsmiths, was actually Latour's research assistant during his stay at the LSE. He also served as her co-supervisor for her doctoral thesis. With her background in pragmatist philosophy and science and technology studies, she was an ideal defender of actor-network theory for the panel. Besides their important contributions on the day, both Introna and Marres had provided some invaluable input into the design of the proceedings during the planning stage, for which we were most grateful.

The composition of the audience was another important concern of ours during the process of designing the format and developing the schedule for the event. While we always intended the symposium to have a relatively small number of participants, in order to allow for an intimate, collegial atmosphere and plenty of audience input, the limited stock of appropriate rooms available at the time of our booking had landed us with the constraint of a maximum of forty-five people. We also knew that due to Bruno Latour's 'rock star' status in the social science community, our problem would not be how to fill up the room with an interested audience, but how not to offend those who would be non-invited or declined. (Fortunately, just the night before the symposium, Latour delivered his open lecture on Gabriel Tarde to a packed house in the

LSE's 450-seat Old Theatre, which took some of the pressure off of us.) As it was mid-December by the time we were in a position to send out invitations, we decided that it was too late to put in place a formal mechanism for inviting applications and thus selecting participants. Instead, we agreed on a personal and professional network-based recruitment strategy, meaning that we would invite people who had been known to us to have a deep-seated interest in either or both of the works of our two authors and who were also geographically relatively close to London, to increase the chances of attendance.

At the same time we were keen to assemble an audience that was as diverse as possible, both in terms of discipline and academic seniority. The recruitment process was managed via email, using an Excel database developed for this purpose, as well as a Google Doc spreadsheet where we collaboratively logged and monitored the distribution of Harman's manuscript. The PDF copy of the manuscript, besides the figure of Bruno Latour, was the other critically important and effective recruitment tool. The audience recruitment process had its own protocol too, built around the manuscript. Invitees were promised a copy of the *Prince of Networks* manuscript upon acceptance of the invitation, which in turn they were requested to read prior to the event. Participants were also given the opportunity to submit questions or comments to the two authors and panel members in advance. This approach had created considerable word-of-mouth advertising for the event, as requests started flooding in from all over the world for copies of Harman's manuscript, especially from PhD students. In the end we were fortunate to attract a multidisciplinary and multinational crowd, representing fields as different as accounting, architecture, English literature, geography, information systems, media studies, sociology and philosophy. The audience spanned the entire academic hierarchy of researchers, from PhD students and junior faculty to professors and heads of department, even including a vice-chancellor in the person of Nigel Thrift.

The setup of the experiment consisted of two sites on the fifth floor of the LSE's Old Building. The Chairman's Dining Room (CDR) was as our 'life-support system,' where refreshments were provided during the registration and after the event, and where lunch was served. During registration delegates received name tags, the schedule, a list of attendees and a leaflet introducing ISIG; they also had a chance to circulate and meet each other. After lunch and at the end of the event the CDR also served as a kind of 'decompression chamber,' where participants could reflect on the discussions in a relaxed manner outside of the laboratory proper, the Graham Wallas Room. The latter was laid out in a traditional panel discussion format, with a long table for the speakers and panelists at the front, facing rows of audience members. The table was clad in an LSE branded cloth and —covering each corner behind the speakers— there were two large roll-up banners displaying ISIG's research foci. This arrangement was finalized by Aleksi, Maha, Ofer and Wifak on the morning of the event. Ofer even managed to extend the 'life-support system' into the Graham Wallas Room, by smuggling in and installing a water cooler next to the speakers' table to keep them rehydrated and lubricate their vocal cords during the grueling three and a half hour long performance.

The appendix contains a copy of the schedule which outlines the proceedings of the event. Nevertheless, the experimental protocol could be said to have started when participants, including Bruno Latour and the panelists, received the PDF copy of Harman's manuscript. This was followed by the reading of the text and formulation of questions and comments, some of which were submitted via email in advance (also in the appendix) or brought along to be asked in person formally or informally. After Leslie Willcocks's welcome (as the Head of ISIG) and Edgar Whitley's introduction (as the symposium chair), Graham Harman made the first presentation by summarizing the main points of his manuscript, which in effect was an evaluation and critique of Bruno Latour's philosophy. Next it was Bruno Latour's turn to respond to

Harman's interpretation, after which Harman was given an opportunity to reply. These structured presentations and responses
eventually gave way to a more *ad hoc* back-and-forth discussion
between the two. The final part of this 2-hour session was taken up
by Harman and Latour answering questions posed by the audience
and the panelists.

Informal discussions naturally continued among smaller
groups of participants in the 'decompression chamber' during
lunch. After the 45-minute lunch break, the second half of the event
began, which was driven by our two panelists, Lucas Introna and
Noortje Marres. Their role was to reignite the debate by picking up
on the most contested issues that emerged in the morning
discussion to ensure that no pressing questions went unanswered,
while also presenting their own take on Harman's manuscript. As
part of the panel discussion, the floor was then opened up for
questions from the audience once more. While according to the
schedule the event was supposed to conclude with the formal
closing statements by both of our main speakers, we agreed
beforehand to deviate from this format if the panel discussion
maintained its momentum, which it did. After an hour and twenty
minutes, when we reached the planned closing time, the chair
brought the proceedings to an end. Some of the conversations
nevertheless continued informally as the participants helped
themselves to refreshments in the Chairman's Dining Room, before
bidding farewell to each other. As soon as the last participant
exited, the organizers started to take apart the set and rearrange the
Graham Wallas Room, in order to return it to its original state as a
classroom for the next users.

The preceding description of the laboratory setup and the
experimental protocol may seem rather mundane and even banal.
To a large extent, it was indeed the mundane and banal delibera-
tions and undertakings that took up most of the organizers' time
for several months, during which this format had gradually
evolved and all the necessary elements assembled into the thing

that the symposium eventually became. This construction process was far from being a smooth teleological emergence though, as it had its crises, stresses and uncertainties until the very end. We, the student organizers, were all very excited about the prospects of this experiment and what it might contribute to our doctoral dissertations, but we were also filled with doubt due to the risks we were facing. What if the experiment fails? What if we won't find out what we hoped to learn? What if for one reason or another one of the actors pulls out? What if the wolf devours the prince? What if the prince skins the wolf alive? Shouldn't we each be getting on with our own PhD projects instead of spending three months organizing an event? Despite all these risks, the prospect of the shower of sparks emanating from the experiment and illuminating our various metaphysical problems was so tantalizing that we were drawn to the inevitable dénouement like so many moths.

Even Pasteur's microbes managed to enter the fray when, just a few days before the event, they inflicted a terrible throat infection upon Graham Harman at the very start of his UK speaking tour. To his credit he fought the microbes heroically, and armed with some pharmacological ammunition, in a daze, grimacing with pain, he delivered his Bournemouth lectures on Heidegger's "Origin of the Work of Art" and Marshall McLuhan's tetrad to general acclaim.[22] As he was dozing off on the Bournemouth-to-London train on the afternoon of February 4, exhausted from his McLuhan talk and gathering strength for Latour's LSE lecture in the evening and the debate the day after, sitting right next to him, I was overcome by an eerie feeling. This thing, this creature — the symposium — suddenly felt real and independent. As its lead organizer, I felt superfluous. "I could be run over by a car now," I mused, "and it would probably still go ahead."

But we made it to the event safely, and it ran without a hitch (if we discount the false fire alarm in a neighboring building which fortunately our speakers didn't seem to notice in the heat of the discussion).[23] We couldn't have asked for a more exciting, informative and entertaining debate; it was a heady mix of metaphysics and methodology, peppered with outbursts of hearty laughter. Hearing Bruno Latour howl like a wolf was priceless. Besides all the fun, a lot of learning naturally also took place for everyone involved. Bruno Latour learned that he is a secular occasionalist and a serial re-describer. Graham Harman learned that objects are vectors for Latour and that Latour rejects Harman's reading of his philosophy as punctualism. The audience learned that in some respects Latour considers himself an old-fashioned positivist and a Darwinian philosopher. In his introduction, Leslie Willcocks joked that in this case Latour won't be able to recall his ideas (in the way manufacturers recall their faulty products),[24] thanks to the materiality of Harman's manuscript. But Latour astonished everyone by 'recalling' some of his most famous and successful ideas, including the concept of network, the principle of irreduction, and the link between his ontology and politics.

In our miniature 'particle accelerator', the repeated clashes between our two philosopher-objects had generated far more sparks than any one of us could have possibly captured and interpreted at the time when it was all happening. For this reason we had three different digital voice recorders recording the event. We decided against filming, as we didn't want the camera's gaze to make our speakers and panelists more self-conscious and reserved to the detriment of the experiment. As it turned out, even repeatedly listening to the recordings was no guarantee of easily being able to access the debate. The Information Systems and Innovation Group had very generously sponsored the transcription of the recording by a professional transcription service. Alas, the ANT principle of translation has plentifully manifested itself in the resulting artifact, as the script remained largely impenetrable thanks to the complex theoretical character of the debate and the various accents which the transcribers often failed to decipher. They repeatedly asked to renegotiate the fee and extend the deadline as the complexity of the task gradually dawned on them.

While the initial transcript was still a good starting point, it took me a month of work listening to the recording at various speeds countless times before most of the gaps were filled and the inconsistencies were ironed out. The output of the 'particle accelerator' began to make sense only when it was slowed down to 50% of its speed. Relevant sections of the transcript were then emailed to all contributors for review, as a courtesy but also as a quality control measure. The transcript went through a final round of editing where the text was adjusted in order to make it more readable and comprehensible for visual consumption. By the end of the process I was completely convinced that transcription is just another form of translation and that it would not only be impossible but also pointless to construct a transcript that would be 100% accurate, as the final editing allowed for the reconstruction of sentences that otherwise would have languished in a fragmented and larval form in the literal transcript.

In the meantime the digital recording of the event began to take on a life of its own. Copies of the file were posted on the LSE website and the ANTHEM blog.[25] On the latter, the file had been accessed over 1,300 times between February 2008 and September 2009, and presumably even more often on the LSE website. To this day, the post containing the links to the recordings is the most popular one on the ANTHEM blog and it continues to be accessed daily. The popularity of the recording was one important factor prompting us to consider the transcript for publication. The other was the desire to process the event, to understand it, to turn it into a reference that can propel our own work one way or another.

While the digital files continued to transmit the Harman-Latour debate across the blogosphere and across the globe, the Harman Review experience also had some curious effects on our two protagonists. Around the time of the symposium Graham Harman emailed his manuscript in PDF form to over 150 people who requested it, before he stopped counting. The circulation of the digital artifact begot more and more requests for copies of it. It was adopted as required reading for various courses at universities such as Berkeley, Brown, Columbia, Guelph, and NYU, even before Harman managed to find a publisher. His positive experience with digital artifacts mediating his ideas must have been a determining factor in his decision to publish *Prince of Networks* with the Australian open access publisher re.press, which produced it both as a standard paperback book and as a freely downloadable e-book. It did not take long before Harman and Latour joined the Apostles of open access publishing, by becoming editors of the New Metaphysics book series at Open Humanities Press.

It is not too hard to see that the symposium was a heterogeneous gathering, a constructed thing, which went on thinging, producing other things. Besides the aforementioned effects, it informed the revision of Harman's manuscript and the completion of the crucial final chapter, "Object-Oriented Philosophy", which makes up a third of his book. It is not inconceivable that the symposium together with Harman's book also had some effects on Latour's work-in-progress manuscript on "the modes of existence." And we could include our humble doctoral theses in their various states of completion in this list. But it would be wrong to focus exclusively on tangible outputs here: our workshop was just as much involved in the making of two philosophers, in the construction of two philosophies.

The most obvious tangible materialization of the symposium, however, is this present book. If you accept the laboratory metaphor, then this artifact you are now holding in your hands is a direct outcome of our experiment. In *Laboratory Life*, Bruno Latour and Steve Woolgar define laboratory activity as "the organization of persuasion through literary inscription."[26] Literary inscription isn't just a linguistic operation; instead it is the transposition, or rather translation of meaning and being from one mode of existence (that of a complex molecule for instance) to another mode of existence: that of a literature reference in a science journal. According to Latour and Woolgar this process of scientific fact construction requires the use of what they call "inscription devices," complex arrangements of laboratory apparatus, which "transform pieces of matter into written documents."[27] This foreword is meant to serve as a description of the "inscription device" that was involved in producing this particular text. While our inscription device was incomparably simpler than the ones used in Roger Guillemin's laboratory —it might be even more appropriate to describe it as a "transcription device"— it was nonetheless engaged in the construction of facts, in our case the facts of social science methodology and metaphysics.

I have deliberately abstained from passing judgments about the quality of the outcome of the experiment in this description. In my multiple roles as 'laboratory scientist,' 'resident anthropologist,' and 'intended consumer' of the resulting scientific text I am already too deeply implicated in this story to credibly feign any sort of impartiality. Instead let me offer the above account of the setup and operation of the apparatus which produced this text as a tool that will hopefully facilitate the assessment of this experiment. Did the prince, armed with the advice of Machiavelli, get the better of the wolf? Did he manage to slip away? Or was it the wolf who emerged victorious? Perhaps I am not giving away too much if I reveal that the prince and the wolf got along amicably. But as for the ending of this fairy tale, I invite you, Dear Reader, to appraise it for yourself.

Peter Erdélyi
September 2009

The transcript of
"The Harman Review: Bruno Latour's Empirical Metaphysics" symposium at the LSE on February 5, 2008

Leslie Willcocks

Welcome to this workshop on behalf of the Information Systems and Innovation Group here at the London School of Economics and Political Science. Our group researches a range of areas in regard to information and communication technologies– I would mention by way of example innovation and technology, information technology (IT) for development and in the public sphere, the sourcing of IT services, health care information systems, information privacy and security, mobile and new technologies, IT development processes, and the management of IT. However, common to these endeavors is a central focus on the social study of information and communication technologies. In terms of publication this concern is best represented by two books, one edited by Claudio Ciborra, Chrisanthi Avgerou and Frank Land called *The Social Study of Information and Communication Technologies*,[28] in which there appears both Bruno Latour and "A (Somewhat) Socratic Dialogue" on ANT, and the other *Social Theory and Philosophy for Information Systems*, which is an edited book I did with John Mingers.[29] These give you a flavor for how we feel— that social theory and philosophy should not be marginalized as they so often are in the Information Systems field, but need to be placed at the core of trying to understand information and communication technologies.

Certainly our PhD program comes up time and again with a lot of philosophy at the heart of PhD proposals, which brings me on to the first person I need to mention, Peter Erdélyi, who is the inspiration for this event. I knew I was into something interesting when I was reading his PhD major upgrade document and found on an early page a matrix that consisted of Heidegger's fourfold which he was going to use to analyze informating ICTs in small and medium enterprises [LAUGHTER]. From which you might assess that Peter is rather good at synthesis. And he also became extremely interested in Graham Harman's work and the synthesis between Heidegger, Latour and Graham Harman. And that is why we are in this fragile position today talking about the metaphysics of the Prince of Networks: Bruno Latour.

The second person I would need to mention is Bruno Latour himself. I am not going to repeat any plaudits for Bruno. You know his work even better than I, I suspect. One thing I do know about Bruno is that he has a very good sense of humor, which I hope will come to the fore today. I remember back in Cambridge, in 1996, when he was asked about actor-network theory and he remarked that he wishes that ideas could have the same recall notice that Ford Motor cars had when they are faulty. But alas, ideas can't have recall notices and unfortunately Bruno, today, because of the work of Graham Harman, I suspect your ideas on metaphysics don't have recall notices either because there is a rather permanent text here that's been written. I'm sure Graham will explain why he has called Bruno the *prince* of networks and not the emperor or king, later on. I am sure there is a rationale for that. The major debate, I think, is going to be around this manuscript today. I've read it. I have found it delightful and easy to read, which I can't always say about books on metaphysics or books on Bruno Latour [LAUGHS].

So that brings us to the last subject (or is it object?) that I need to mention, which is metaphysics itself. I was thinking, how do you introduce the subject of metaphysics? And I went back to one of my favorite films as a boy, which was called Scaramouche. You might recall this film, which has Stewart Granger in it. To revenge a terrible family wrong, he decides he is going to have to become the best fencer in France. And so he is in training for this and a man is training him to fence and he knocks the sword out of his hand. What's the learning point about that? Well the learning point is that according to this fencing master, a sword is like a little bird. If you hold it too tightly, you crush it; if you hold it too loosely, it flies away. And I suspect metaphysics is a bit like that, and hopefully that's the dilemma we are going to have over the next 3 or 4 hours, when we talk about *Prince of Networks: Bruno Latour and Metaphysics*. I'll hand over to Edgar.

Edgar Whitley

OK. Thank you very much, Leslie, for that introduction both to the group and to the event. My role is the unenviable one of trying to keep these two gentlemen to an approximate time constraint. Our main time constraint is lunch. Those of you who were there for Bruno's talk last night[30] will recall that he got about two-thirds of the way through his presentation, so I will try to keep both speakers approximately to their time (subject to lunch) and to finishing at the end of the session. Just as Leslie suggested, the format involves a discussion of Graham's review of Bruno's empirical metaphysics. So we'll start with Graham presenting the key themes of the book. Bruno will have a chance to respond, Graham will reply, and then we will open it up to audience questions, comments, and discussion.

I know that a number of you have already forwarded particular questions that the speakers and the panelists have had a chance to look at and think about [see Appendix]. Some of those questions might be addressed explicitly in the presentations or raised in the audience questions. And if not, then we've also asked the panelists for the discussion after lunch to deal with any of these particular questions that might still be remaining and to which people might want answers.

Graham Harman

Maybe first I will address the questions about the title of the book and the status of the manuscript. As you may have noticed, the final chapter is missing, and that's not accidental. I deliberately chose to wait until after this event to write the last chapter. Some

23

things you say today could make a contribution to the manuscript, which is already under review by a publisher. But I am still going to make quite a few changes to it.

"King of Networks" was the title of the first paper I ever wrote about Bruno Latour.[31] This was a talk I gave in Chicago almost nine years ago and one of the audience members said afterwards: "You ought to send the paper to Latour himself. Sometimes you'll be surprised, and these authors will respond." And I did send the lecture to Bruno and received a wonderful response, and thus began our correspondence. But when I tried to use this title for the book manuscript, there were a lot of jokes about the film "King of New York," and I decided I would rather not deal with any of those jokes when the book was out. And so then it was a choice between "emperor" and "prince," and emperor is simply too polysyllabic. [LAUGHTER] I didn't think Bruno would view prince as a downgrade from king. The word "prince" also hints at Machiavelli's book, and "Prince of Networks" sounds enough like "Prince of Darkness" [LAUGHTER] to be flattering in a backhanded way.

Above all I would like to thank everyone from ANTHEM who made this happen. ANTHEM stands for Actor-Network-Theory - Heidegger Meeting, which is a great acronym. This is a good match for me, because while half of my head belongs to Latour and half belongs to Heidegger and phenomenology, the two usually do not go together. In fact, until I met the members of ANTHEM, some people thought I was unique or quirky in some sense, and it was a pleasure to discover that others are as quirky as I am. Peter doesn't know this, but I checked this morning, and since August 2007 we have exchanged a total of 796 emails [LAUGHTER], many of them about this event. That's more than four emails per day. He's one of the few people who likes discussing these things by email as much as I do.

The last preliminary remark I wanted to make is that the date of this conference has a lovely symmetry for me because

February of 1988, that's twenty years ago, is when I became a Heideggerian...

Bruno Latour

Today? This specific day? [LAUGHTER].

Graham Harman

No, I don't remember the specific day. I know it was late February. [LAUGHTER] February of 1998 was when I became a Latourian, and here we are today, ten years after that. And of course I would have been delighted back then if I could have looked ten years into the future and seen what was coming today. Also, I wouldn't trade Bruno Latour's presence here today for Martin Heidegger's. Bruno is a much nicer man. [LAUGHTER] He's much funnier as well as a better interlocutor, I'm sure.

Since Heidegger lies in the background of this manuscript, we might ask: what draws a Heideggerian to Latour? In my case at least, Heidegger's *weaknesses* are what drew me to Latour, because he does not share those particular weaknesses. Above all, despite my many years of enthusiasm for Heidegger, his tone was always unbearable to me. For me that tone was merely something to be endured: a kind of grim piety, with a sort of oracular heaviness that is found in all of Heidegger's work. I always appreciated the depth of Heidegger, but never appreciated the rhetorical tone. By contrast, as Leslie already mentioned, Bruno is probably the funniest contemporary philosopher. Throughout the margins of all my copies of Bruno's books I have written comments such as "laughing" and "ha-ha." And in fact I was talking to Gerard de Vries in Amsterdam, one of the leading Dutch experts on Latour. I asked de Vries what drew him to Latour's work and he said that Bruno and his friends were the only funny people working in philosophy. [LAUGHTER] Many philosophers were bores and he didn't enjoy spending time with them; Bruno was an exception.

But even more importantly than the question of tone, there was the fact that Bruno's philosophy is almost the only one of the past century that takes individual objects seriously. Individual objects play a role in his philosophy. In Heidegger that isn't the case because individual objects are dismissed as merely "ontic." What is real is the depth behind the present-at-hand configurations of objects. In Husserl you do find individual things. But they are just phenomena in consciousness, and they don't really do anything. In other contemporary philosophies you'll find that the role of the object is minimized: objects don't play any significant role. One of my favorite moments when we brought Bruno to Egypt in 2003 was his lecture on how the price of apricots in Paris is determined, which I cannot imagine Heidegger or most others attempting as a philosophical topic.

So, what *are* individual things for Bruno Latour? We need to look at *Irreductions,* one of his most underread books, which is often hidden from view because it's not a book in its own right, but a large appendix to his book on Pasteur.[32] And when I first contacted Bruno about the *Prince of Networks* project three or four years ago and told him what I had in mind, he said that any discussion of his philosophy must begin with *Irreductions.* To my surprise, he said it has never been reviewed once, even now. And though *Prince of Networks* cannot really be called an "authorized" book, because I think he disagrees with much of it, the structure of the manuscript was determined by Bruno Latour himself. He is the one who first made me seriously consider that *Irreductions* should provide the impetus for the entire book. And it now is, which is Bruno's own fault. And as stated in my manuscript, there are probably four major concepts in *Irreductions.*

First there is *irreduction* itself, which he presents with his wonderful "Paul on the road to Damascus" anecdote. I'm referring to the sudden revelation he had when he was 24 or 25 years old, and as he tells us he was driving his van on the road between Dijon and Gray and had to pull to the side of the road. He actually went back and found his diary entry from the time and typed it up for me. It was a very dramatic moment, when he decided that what most theories shares in common is a desire to reduce things to something else. Most theories take some primary reality that explains the others and then use that to explain the rest. Latour decided to reject this notion at a young age. And by the way, this also makes him the ally of Heidegger's critique of ontotheology: the notion that any particular *kind* of being can explain being itself. So there's one link between Latour and Heidegger.

Second, we have *actors*, probably the most important concept of his philosophy. Actors are obviously different from traditional substances, the most famous version of objects in the history of philosophy. Actors come in all sizes. The London School of Economics can be an actor, and so can an atom or a piece of paper. Latour is not distinguishing between substance and aggregates the way that Leibniz did, where a circle of men holding hands cannot possibly be a substance because it is merely an aggregate of many individuals. For Latour every individual is already an aggregate to begin with. We heard this again in his nice lecture last night on Gabriel Tarde. So it cannot be said that an actor is simple; it can be of any size. It doesn't have to endure: in fact actors do not endure for him at all, but it certainly doesn't matter that they're not eternal, though classical substances were usually supposed to be eternal. Also, the difference for Latour between real and unreal is not important. Harry Potter can be an actor just as much as a pillar of granite. Anything that has an effect on other things is an actor, and hence there's no difference between physical and non-physical actors. Each actor is a black box containing other actors *ad infinitum*, and all actors are equally real.

But the third point, *alliances*, tells us that if all actors are equally real, not all are equally strong. The fact that an actor is real does not mean that it is just as convincing as the others. Latour is not a relativist: anything does not go. Some actors are very weak; not much proof can be mustered on their behalf, not many allies rush to their aid. But some actors are very strong, because other allies recognize them as real, respond to them, and alter their trajectories to adapt to them.

And finally we have *translation*, the idea that one thing can never be fully translated into another place or time. There is always going to be information loss, or energy loss. You have to pay a price when translating something from one place to another. This is especially wonderful in his brilliant alternative model of truth, which I don't think we've ever seen before from any philosopher. Usually there are disputes between the "correspondence" version of truth where the mind is copying the world, and the "coherence" view of truth where what matters is that your views are consistent with each other. But what we find in Bruno Latour, in *Pandora's Hope*,[33] is an "industrial" model of truth, one of my favorite notions in his work. In order to move the oil trapped in the geological seams of Saudi Arabia to the gas tank in France, you're not "copying" the oil, and neither is it just coherence. I mean, there is a real thing there that has to be translated at each stage. I'm afraid I don't even know all of these stages, but you have to refine it into petrol somehow (I don't know how that happens), then put it on a ship and take it to Europe, and finally it has to be sold to the customer and be put into the gas tank. And if you think of truth as this sort of process, it opens new possibilities for philosophy.

The other thing about actors for Latour is that there is no hidden essence or potential in them. You cannot say that the actors have some hidden inner kernel which is more important than their accidental crust. Actors contain *all* of their features. An actor simply is what it is, which means that an actor contains all of its qualities, or contains all of its relations with other actors. There is nothing hiding behind those qualities and relations. An actor is wholly deployed in the world in every second. There's no cryptic reservoir hiding behind what the thing is doing here and now, what qualities it has here and now. The reality of the actor is its way of perturbing, transforming, and jostling other things.

Now, here's the paradox. And by paradox I don't mean contradiction: I don't mean "Gotcha!" A philosophy is real only when it contains a central paradox. Who was it who said that paradox is the mark of truth? I think it was Count Yorck as quoted by Heidegger in *Being and Time*. And Aristotle even says that substance is that which can have different qualities at different times. So, something is more substantial the more it is capable of paradoxical properties. On the one hand, Latour is clearly a philosopher of relations. His whole philosophy is about relations: the way that things interact, the way they form networks, alliances, and relations. And yet, since everything happens in one time and one place only, and every actor is utterly concrete, this means that actors are completely cut off from each other as well. Everything is completely cut off in its own self, and as we will see in a moment, it can't possibly endure from one instant to the next because it's so utterly concrete that even the smallest change essentially makes it a new actor: unless some other actor does work to establish that the change wasn't important and it's actually still the same thing. But another actor is required to do that. Nothing endures; everything is in a state of perpetual perishing. It's a lot like Whitehead, and also a lot like the occasionalists, and I'll come to that point shortly. Actually, I'm going to it right now: I didn't realize it was my next notecard.

There's a growing tendency to hear people speak of a school of "process philosophy," and you'll sometimes hear Whitehead, Bergson, Deleuze, and Latour grouped together. And I can see why, because what all of those names have in common is that they don't accept the traditional models of substance. That's true. However, it's also a bit sloppy to put those names together, for a reason that becomes pretty obvious if you look at the underpinnings of their philosophies. You have to put Bruno Latour with Whitehead, if you're going to group names together, because what matters for Latour and Whitehead are individual actors in individual instants.

There is no flux, no becoming, and no *élan vital* as separate realities for Latour and Whitehead. For them, time is produced by actors. Time is a result, not a starting point. It's not an independent force. Individual actors for Bruno create time by doing something irreversible. The example he gave at dinner last night: Fermat's Last Theorem. For many centuries nothing happened, and now it is solved. A cut has been made, something irreversible has happened, time has been created by an actor. Whitehead even emphasizes this point with his terminology. He talks about actual entities, but he also calls them "actual occasions," because an actual entity is frozen in an instant. Once it is altered, it's not really the same thing anymore. You can try to find enduring entities in Whitehead at the higher level of societies. But when you talk about actual entities, they are always perishing. In a famous and wonderful phrase, Whitehead tells us that actual entities do not undergo adventures in space and time. They exist in one place and time only, just as for Bruno.

Let me go back and say a little about the history of occasionalism, because it's a neglected but extremely important movement in the history of philosophy, and I think it is one that still dominates us. (I'm going to write something about this later.) Occasionalism goes back to Islamic philosophy. When people think of occasionalism in philosophy, they usually think of France in the seventeenth century, but it actually goes back to Islamic theology. We find it fairly early in the so-called Ash'arite School, which for theological motives did not want to grant the ability to act to created substances. Only Allah could have the power of creation, and even to cause anything to happen at all. They were so extreme that even to give fire the power to burn cotton was for them a kind of blasphemous presumption. And this is why God had to be introduced as a mediator. God is the mediator for all interactions. And this to me is the key contribution of Islamic philosophy. Every so often we see an attempt to revive Islamic philosophy, and certain texts are retranslated or commented upon. But too often this gets stuck in the rut of just saying: "well, we are indebted to the Arabs for keeping Aristotle alive," or something like that. But the main contribution of Islam is that occasionalism entered the very heart of Western philosophy. It took it awhile to get to the West. Notice that for Aristotle and his tradition, causation itself isn't really a *problem*; there are no gaps between things. I mean, he has the four causes— final, formal, efficient, material—but it's not really a problem for Aristotle that one thing can touch another. It took a theological motive to ask how one thing can touch another at all. And the answer was that this is impossible: God must be the mediator.

For Descartes, the motivation is different. His motive is that you have two different kinds of substances, the mind and the body. The only way for the mind to cause the body to move would be for God to serve as the mediator between them. But that's less interesting than the Muslim position on occasionalism, because less universal. But the wider Islamic version of occasionalism was brought back by Cordemoy and Malebranche, for whom the interaction between *bodies* is already a problem again. That's because they brought back individual physical bodies, which Descartes rejected. And for Cordemoy the interaction of physical atoms requires God's mediation as well. And I would go so far as to say that the term "occasionalism" is used far too restrictively. Sometimes historians get touchy about this. They want to restrict it only to Malebranche and a few others, and don't even want to include Descartes. I would call most of the seventeenth century figures occasionalists, including Leibniz, Spinoza, Berkeley. And I think it's fairly clearly the dominant trend in seventeenth century metaphysics. Of course no one takes occasionalism seriously anymore. It seems like a very dated theology, and it's fun for undergraduates to refute it in intro-ductory classes. The exception of course is Whitehead, who takes pride in starting *Process and Reality* by saying: "Let's forget about Kant and go back to the Seventeenth Century." And then he is able to walk freely among all these philosophies, and take occasion-alism seriously.

But what is not laughed at today is skepticism, and Kant has a solution to skepticism. Skepticism is in many ways still the horizon of contemporary philosophy and so it's taken seriously, at least in the back of almost everyone's mind. And if you think about it, skepticism is really just an upside-down version of occasionalism. You've got the same problem in both cases: how can one thing necessarily connect with another? In a way these two are just the inverse of one another, and here it is interesting to note that Hume was a great fan of Malebranche, and was deeply inspired by him. In occasionalism the problem is that you have individual substances, you know these substances can exist. But how can they touch? It would be blasphemous to allow them to touch, so it must be God who's allowing them to do so. God comes in as the solution to link substances. In a way, what you have with Hume is that you're simply starting with the relations: things are already related by habit and custom. I already do link these impressions together. The problem is how we know that they can exist independently of such links. How can we know that they have independent powers outside of my habitual linking of them? We can't. So in a way the human mind, or habit, or custom are simply playing the role for Hume that God plays for all the occasionalists. So people can laugh at occasionalism all they want, but most contemporary philosophy is simply adopting the converse solution. So they shouldn't be laughing. Instead, they should be trying to reform their own opposing position.

Now, the problem with both of these theories is that they share the same flaw. Both start off by problematizing relation, specifically causal relation. There's a problem of how two things can relate to each other. And both positions cheat. They both solve the problem falsely by imagining one privileged super-entity that solves the problem. For the occasionalists nothing can touch, but God is an exception. For Hume nothing can touch, but they're already linked in the human mind by habit, so it doesn't matter. So in a sense both are shying away from the abyss: the problem of how two things interact at all. And so I would say that most post-Kantian philosophy is simply an upside-down occasionalism, insofar as it's restricting itself to human access to things and not talking about the interaction of things themselves. Whitehead is of course the permanent exception to most of the rules of post-Kantian philosophy. He begins *Process and Reality* by simply saying "Let's go back to the 17th Century; philosophy has gone downhill since Kant." And how do things communicate for Whitehead? Things are actual entities and they are fully defined by their relations to other things, which he calls *prehensions*. But how do they prehend each other? Well, they prehend each other through the eternal objects, which can roughly be described as Platonic forms. Things oversimplify each other when they prehend each other through these... universal qualities, you could call them. And these universal qualities have to be somewhere. Where are they? For Whitehead they are in God. So it's the same solution, the old occasionalist solution. And it is very refreshing compared to most recent philosophy, but still has the same problem of bringing in a sort of magical solution at the end.

And I happen to think that this is the greatness of Latour as a metaphysician. I think he has made a real breakthrough in being the first person to problematize relations and not employ one of these magical last-ditch solutions. He's not from the Kantian tradition and so he doesn't put everything in the human mind. He doesn't follow Whitehead in utilizing God to serve this particular causal role in his philosophy. Latour's philosophy is a kind of secular occasionalism, and we've never seen that before. It's a philosophy where you have to ask how things interact on a local level without appealing to some all-powerful super-entity that's hidden somewhere from us. He does not flee from the problem of translation, but makes it the central theme of his philosophy.

All relation for Latour requires a mediator. Any two things *can* be linked, but only if something links them. In perhaps his most wonderful example, politics and neutrons can be linked, but only if Joliot in France links them: only if he's able to convince the French government that neutrons are part of a good defense policy, and only if he is able to convince neutrons to participate by designing experiments in the right way to give the sorts of results that are plausible enough to make a working bomb. It's not God who links politics and neutrons, and it's not the human mind that links them. It's Joliot. And every actor is a kind of Joliot. Any entity can link any two other entities, and so a local occasionalism must be possible.

We know that Bruno Latour is a philosopher of actors and networks. We can rewrite this to say that he is a philosopher of objects and relations (those are the terms I prefer to use). His actors are objects of all sizes; they can be either real or unreal in physical terms; they are black boxes that you can open to find many more actors hidden within them; and every actor has effects on other entities. And as for relations, we know from Latour's philosophy that their link is only occasional: they need a third term or mediator, something that links them. And for these reasons I will always be a Latourian, no matter how much he might not like certain parts of the second half of my book. I will always have this Latourian base in my philosophy because Heidegger doesn't give me any of these things. Heidegger pays no real attention to objects at all, and Latour's kind of relation isn't really found in Heidegger, since human *Dasein* is the one doing all the relating. And furthermore, Latour has launched a style of philosophy (secular occasionalism) that's completely unavailable elsewhere. You're not going to find it even in Whitehead, because there's always an appeal to the eternal objects and to God. Whitehead is not going to look the problem of relations squarely in the face. And of course Bruno does this with a wit and liveliness that are well worth emulating, just as Heidegger's tone is worth avoiding.

And I will now select four of the things I said in the second half of the book that I think need to be worked on to make the philosophy of objects and relations feasible. One of them is that given that any two actors can only be linked through a mediator, there's the possible problem of an infinite regress. If Joliot is required to link neutrons and politics, what links Joliot and neutrons, and what links Joliot and politics? Well, you could say that Joliot's eyeballs link him with the neutrons, or that his training in physics links him with the neutrons, and you could say that that's not so interesting so we don't have to consider it. Yes, if you are simply trying to give an analysis of Joliot's life, you could say that for all practical purposes it's not very interesting to know what lies between Joliot and politics or neutrons, and so we can avoid the question. But in metaphysical terms, there is a problem here. You have to explain how any two things can be linked. And for this reason there must be a space where direct contact is possible without mediation. We need to discover what that space is where links are possible.

Okay, points 2 and 3 come from my phenomenological background, which Bruno Latour does not share. One of them is that my Heideggerian side makes me resist the idea that objects can be made up of relations. This is an unorthodox reading of Heidegger, of course. But the way I read Heidegger's tool-analysis... Let me summarize this quickly because maybe not everyone here is familiar with Heidegger. I think I have maybe a few more minutes? Okay.

Heidegger's tool-analysis is meant as a critique of Husserl, who was Heidegger's great teacher. Husserl's goal can roughly be described as protecting philosophy from the growing advance of the natural sciences. Philosophy in the late 1800s was in danger of becoming experimental psychology. And Husserl's way of preventing this from happening was to say that all these physical theories are just theories. If you hear a door slam, you can invent a theory about vibrations going through the air and coming into your ear and vibrating your eardrum and sending chemical signals up the nervous system, but we don't really have any direct access to that. Those theories are grounded in my *experience* of the door slamming. So what we should do instead is simply describe what it's like to hear the door slam: what I'm actually hearing, what I'm inferring, and what the different layers of sound are to which I might not normally be paying attention. This is what phenomenological description is about, and it's often accused of becoming a kind of psychology in its own right, and to some extent it does verge on psychology.

Heidegger's attack on this position was simply to say that our normal interaction with things is not phenomenal, not as images in consciousness. We take things for granted; we use them; we rely on things. Our consciousness is a very small percentage of our interaction with things at any moment. You're using the floor now to support you; you're using the oxygen in the room to breathe; you're using your bodily organs to keep you alive. And most of the time you're not thinking about these things unless they break. And so Heidegger's famous tool-analysis in *Being and Time* talks about the "disturbance of reference" when things malfunction or fail in some way, and come to our attention in a way that they didn't before. They emerge from shadow into light. And they don't actually have to break for this happen. You can do this with theoretical consciousness. You can do this simply by talking about something or noticing something. All these different ways show that for Heidegger there's something hidden behind all of our theories or our seeing; there's a deeper layer.

Now, it is sometimes said that this means that "practice comes before theory for Heidegger; Heidegger is a pragmatist." No, this is not true, because notice that even our practical use of things does not exhaust them. By sitting on the chair you're also not coming into contact with all the properties of the chair. The chair has many different qualities that your sitting in it does not exhaust any more than your looking at the chair does. There are tiny electromagnetic vibrations coming off the chair that certain insects might be able to perceive though you cannot, and they're completely irrelevant to us as humans. But the chair seems to have an infinity of these qualities that no other entity will ever unlock. And then you have to take a third step (and I got this from Whitehead actually, even before I knew Bruno's work) and see that things do this to each other as well. Things oversimplify each other just as much as we do. It's not a special property of human consciousness to distort the world. Entities will distort each other *ipso facto* by the mere fact that they relate. For fire to burn cotton, which is the favorite Islamic example discussed in all those ancient texts, fire does not need to react to most of the properties of the cotton: its smell and its color are irrelevant to the fire. The fire is going to burn the cotton based on flammable properties, whatever those are.

And so the object is deeper than any possible relations to it. If you say that an object is reducible to its relations with other things, which I know Bruno believes, I think a couple of other problems arise. One problem is that I don't think you can explain change. And this is something Aristotle says against the Megarians in the *Metaphysics*. Like Bruno I'm also opposed to "potentiality," but I think there has to be something outside of a thing's relations. If a thing is nothing other than its current relations, then why would it ever change those relations? If I am completely exhausted by my current state of relations to all of the entities in the world, then there's nothing hidden in reserve, nothing cryptic, nothing that would later unfold and give me the chance to have new relations to things. So in a way this position doesn't do justice to my future. And in a way it can't even explain my present, because we can imagine a counterfactual situation in which other people would be sitting in this room who aren't currently here, who would be seeing me from different angles and having different reactions to me than any of you do. And they would still be reacting *to me*, not to your relations to me. So there is something here that is really *me* that these people are all encountering. I'm not just the sum total of the ways that I relate to all of you right now.

Okay, so that's the second point I wanted to make, and I only have two more. The other thing that Bruno does in his philosophy is that he identifies an object with its qualities: not just with its relations but also with its qualities. In his view you cannot say that an object is different from its qualities. Whereas for Husserl (and here's my phenomenological background coming in) I would say that Husserl's primary insight is the distinction between a thing and its qualities. These days people often dismiss Husserl: he's just an idealist, he's taking us back to Descartes and Kant. It's not quite that simple. Yes, Husserl was an idealist; yes, he does suspend the real world from consideration. But notice that when you're reading Husserl, it *feels* like realism. There's a definite taste of realism in your mouth when you're reading Husserl, even though he's an idealist. Now why is that? It's because Husserl is talking about objects. They're simply not real objects that have independent force; they're called intentional objects. To take a famous example, Husserl spent a whole semester having his students analyze a mailbox. You cannot imagine Fichte or Hegel spending a whole semester having their students analyze a mailbox; it would make no sense for them. An object has no opacity and no resistance for these German idealists. It's simply one transient moment of the dialectic and then it's gone; you're already removed to some higher structure. For Husserl, individual objects already have a kind of potency and weight, an obscurity: even though they're not real, and are present only in the human mind. If you circle a building, you keep thinking of it as the same building even though you're seeing utterly different qualities in each instant, which means that there a distinction between the building and the qualities through which it is manifested. Those qualities are almost accidental; you just need to be seeing *some* qualities of the building in order to be able to see it. But you can keep circling the building and it stays the same. It remains identical, even if it's not real: even if it's the Tooth Fairy that you're circling in your mind, the same thing happens.

Now this is important, because this is Husserl's challenge to the entire tradition of British empiricism, whose position is often very much taken for granted: the idea that a thing is nothing more than a bundle of qualities. There's nothing called a thing that's independent of those. Locke says it; Hume says it. There's a tradition of mockery of the "I know not what." When they say "I know not what," it's with a sarcastic tone, since supposedly all that we really know are the qualities. But for Husserl, the objects come first. And for one of his followers, Merleau-Ponty, there are no qualities independent of the thing. If you're looking at ink, a shirt, a flag, the black is different in each of those cases even if it is technically the same shade of black, because it's now impregnated with the underlying object, which is never fully present to you. And on this point Bruno sides with the British empiricists.

There's also a whole debate in the philosophy of language, which has been very central for analytic philosophy. On one side you have Russell and Frege, who uphold the traditional view that a person's name is simply an abbreviation for all the qualities we know about them. And on the opposite side there is Kripke who says, "No, with a name you're pointing at something that's deeper than the qualities." Why? Because I can discover that all the qualities I think I knew about somebody, all the properties I thought I knew about you, were false. What I will say if that happens is, "Oh, I was wrong about everything I thought I knew about you," I'm not going to say "you're a different person." It doesn't matter that the qualities change. I'm still pointing at the same thing: a "rigid designator," he calls it. And you have that in Husserl too, because you're pointing at the same intentional object no matter how the qualities change.

And so to repeat, my first point is that there's an infinite regress of mediators, and that's a problem with Latour's theories of relations. The second and third points were problems with the theory of the actor, possible problems with the theories of actors. Maybe a thing is not the same as its relations, and maybe a thing is not the same as its qualities. And the fourth problem is that, despite Bruno's wonderful career-long assault on Kant, which I cheer every step of the way, we still have not brought back the problems that Kant threw out of philosophy. All of the cosmological problems that were supposedly eliminated forever in the transcendental dialectic, all those traditional metaphysical problems are not back with us. Whitehead picks up on a few of them, Latour picks up on a few of them. Kant thinks it's impossible to know whether or not there's an infinite regress of wholes and parts; Latour tells us there's an infinite regress. You might read him as merely saying that "for all practical purposes" we never know where the last black box is. But I think that if you follow his logic, you have to say the black boxes never stop opening. And so in a way he is asserting a *metaphysical* claim that there is no final atom that will be an unopenable box. And so I would think we also need to be a little more ambitious about going right at the cyclops eye of Kant in trying to save all of these problems that were cancelled in the second half of *The Critique of Pure Reason*. And we see a few people trying this now from various different angles. In Meillassoux's book[34] we see an attempt to tackle some of these cancelled Kantian problems as well, and he's coming from a totally different angle from mine.

So, what I've tried to do in this opening summary is talk about what I consider to be the key concepts of Latour's metaphysics, the key things that I appreciate about it, and also some reservations that I have that stem mostly from my Heidegger/ Husserl background. And I know some of his reactions to these points, because we've had a few email exchanges. But perhaps he would like to spell out some of his reactions today.

Edgar Whitley
Thank you, Graham.

[APPLAUSE]

Bruno Latour
Thank you, Graham. Thank you, Edgar. Thank you, Peter and the

ANTHEM Group. I'll try to be shorter than my allotted time so that we have time for a rejoinder and to discuss. I am not going to answer the four questions which were raised by Graham because I don't have the answers to them. Actually I'm not sure I have a metaphysics, so let me make two remarks as a sort of a user's manual of my argument.

The difficulty for me is that I am not a professional philosopher of course, and when I speak of "empirical metaphysics," the word *empirical* is more important for me than the word *metaphysical*. In other words, I'm like a dog following its prey, and then the prey arrives in the middle of a band of wolves which are called professional philosophers [LAUGHTER]. But I am actually following the prey. My intention was not to fall in with the wolves and to have to answer all of these guys while trying to catch my prey.

I am being slightly disingenuous here, because I am also interested in leading the dog somewhere. But the exercise of doing metaphysics is what I'm uncomfortable with in your book. I mean, for an author it's marvelous to be compared with all these big figures, and even though I'm not delusional enough to believe all that you've said about what I've done, it is of course very nice. But it doesn't mean that it's true [LAUGHTER]. At one point you very nicely say that Latour's presence in the network of his own philosophy is actually peripheral. So I'm perfectly comfortable here in discussing your book that discusses my books. I'm just one of the authors in the network, and not necessarily the best one to interpret your book. And actually as Foucault said, I'm probably not the *best* to talk about my own work [LAUGHS]. The author has no real privilege.

But there are two points where I feel some distance from your book. One is that it's a kind of voiceover for me, a moment when I write a metaphysical voiceover to talk about some empirical matter which interests me most. And here we disagree in point of style, because you are not a sociologist or anthropologist and you are more interested in the voiceover itself.

But to take just *Irreductions* for example, it's just half of the Pasteur project, and for me it's a binary weapon, and if you don't put the two chemicals together then in a way it has no effect. And the same is true of *Aramis*[35] and the same of *The Making of Law*[36] and so on. So, all of these works are of a very different status. And I think that the big philosophers you mention are homogeneously serious, so to speak, and I'm not homogeneously serious because it depends entirely on the task at hand.

So the second point where we may differ slightly is that I think we need an experimental apparatus, so to speak, to have a discussion. And today the experimental apparatus which has been organized is a comparison between Heidegger and myself, but I'm out of the loop here because I don't know enough about Heidegger and certainly not as much as you do. But there are other experimental apparatuses, and when I was privileged to be in this department here, in Information Systems at the LSE, it was another experimental device. We tried to see if it makes a difference if information is modified, if the meaning of infor-mation is modified for doing empirical studies about many of the things that are done in this department. So I'm slightly embar-rassed for a third reason, which is that I disagree with most of what I've written myself [LAUGHTER], and I will explain that in a moment.

So I agree with a lot of things you said about *Irreductions* and I think you made a marvelous and very witty [LAUGHS] point about getting out of the counter-Copernican revolution and escaping the duality of human and nonhuman things. And given the fact that even many of my friends in sociology are still stuck with this human-nonhuman opposition, you prove that the philosophers get it much faster than the social sciences, and for that I'm very grateful. I think I'm also beginning to like the word "occasionalism" [LAUGHS] and even vicarious occasionalism. And I like this idea that it has some completely unknown connection with the philosophy and theology of Islam.

But I have two sorts of problems. The first is that I don't understand the question you keep asking... basically I prefer the first part
of the book to the second part for some reason [LAUGHTER]. The
more the book goes on, the more you impose, in my view, a
problem that I still don't get. Still, the final chapter is not there yet
and your solution to the problem you pose is still not visible, and
it's difficult for me to see. But the problem I don't understand is
that after having said so much, I think correctly, about the fact that
translation is the key problem because of the irreducible singularity of every single object, you accuse me– or not accuse, but in
your hyperbolic and very kind critique you say that I associate
myself with the doctrine that "everything is relational." And that I
don't get, I simply don't get. We've had many exchanges, emails et
cetera over the years and a nice time meeting in Egypt and so on,
and I can see that we are not going to solve this disagreement. But
I don't understand the argument, because for me it's precisely
because of the irreducible singularity (which you sometimes call
the inner kernel of things) that they have to be translated without
ever emptying their kernel. Why I am associated with another
school of philosophy which would reduce things to their relations,
I don't understand. Actually I don't understand what it means to
say that a thing is just its relations, and I've never really understood that. And I don't understand why it is a problem in your
book, since you do such a beautiful job of showing that from the
very beginning the principle of irreduction is precisely to say that
it's always at a cost that you make a relation possible.

And actually it's something that you see in geography as well.
I'm very influenced by Nigel [Thrift] and the geographers more
generally, who have a fabulous metaphor... It's actually because of
the irreducibility of space that you have to get into connections,
that translation is made visible for the social sciences, and that the
task of mediation is visible. So it seems to me, though maybe I'm
wrong here, that in the first part of the book you see the problem
very well, but then you sort of shoehorn it into a problem which

involves an alternative between a thing that would be made of its relations and a thing that would be made of its inner intimacy, and I still have trouble with this because it seems to me that it's precisely because of the principle of irreduction that translation is so important.

The second point I have to make before getting into the second part is that it's very difficult for me to use the word *empirical* as meaning insignificant or disposable detail. And here there is a strong disagreement which is perhaps the heart of the difference between a philosopher and a social scientist. If I take for instance what you say about pragmatism being okay in terms of method but not okay in metaphysics, it means that metaphysics should be able to define the furniture of the world in a sort of coherent way. And you say that if one is an occasionalist (and since you now give me this beautiful name I will accept it) then one has to be an occasionalist all the way. But [LAUGHS] empiricism is not about small details which could be added up by another profession. Empiricism means that the details of the actual occasions are the important theoretical features that we want to detect.

So let's consider this example that takes up a good part of your book, which is this infamous example of Pasteur and the microbe. If you look at the general point about backward causation, it's just a silly argument, and in metaphysical terms I actually will not defend it. I'm very worried that my colleagues in the philosophy department here in this school might see that my name is associated with metaphysics at all, because I think they would be very, very cross [LAUGHTER] that the LSE indulges in that sort of thing [LAUGHTER]. Because if you take it as a metaphysical argument, it's completely ridiculous. But if you follow it in detail, in the fact that Pasteur does modify it in this way, writes the whole history of fermentation from the Egyptians to the invention of wine, etc., very explicitly, by actually writing papers showing that what people had believed before is now explained in terms of microbes, in terms of fermentation, of a ferment that "I Pasteur now demonstrate," then it becomes an interesting point. Because then you see that in this specific instance how Pasteur does solve the question of backward causation. But I agree that taken as a general principle it's very weak, but it's a weakness which is due to the fact that it's a voiceover for a phenomenon which is meant as an important phenomenon, not as a metaphysical voiceover.

This is where I sometimes have difficulty. My whole point about the modernists, all of that was really because no one understood what we are doing in science studies. You see it's not the same thing as describing the furniture of the world, which is a metaphysical question.

And the other question you ask... Let's take armies, a technical project (and no one is interested in technical projects usually). It raises [LAUGHS] a lot of interesting questions no one understands precisely because the continuation in time of a technical project is a big problem, which is not solved by any alluding to materiality in any sense. Because materiality is precisely what is lacking so much in technical projects, as everyone in information systems knows [LAUGHS]. Okay, so here it's a case where the continuation in existence of a project is a complete enigma. No one understands this because they say that the social construction of technology means adding a bit of society to a bit of technology, the social plus the materialism, the worst combination.

Okay, then because you want to understand this very strange entity, you have this very strange ontology which is a project rather than an object, and why don't people understand? And then you realize that the metaphysics you learned in school is still influential in the minds of your readers, especially because they've all read Heidegger. So it's a very different type of production of metaphysical questions when you follow the prey, so to speak, than when you want to establish the basic furniture of the universe. And I have to say, I must sound completely like an old fashioned positivist in the worst sense [LAUGHS]. I think I'm like Auguste Comte in the nineteenth century in that respect, I'm sorry to say

[LAUGHS]. If you want me to speak of the metaphysics where technical projects, religious speech, political enunciations etc., cohabitate, then I'm happy to be a metaphysician. But it's not exactly the same sort of thing.

It's the same with the word *pragmatist*. I know you don't think Dewey is a great philosopher but I think he is a very interesting philosopher precisely because of the *pragmata* and "the thing," of which you speak at the end. So if you are a pragmatist, it doesn't mean there are a few small details that the social sciences would solve while the basic principles and foundations are provided by philosophers. I resent that because I think it's wrong, and that's not the way to collaborate between philosophy and social sciences. Philosophy is too important to be the foundation of the social sciences. Philosophy is the calisthenics necessary to be as subtle as the case at hand. So pragmatism means that we are *pragmata*. And it's quite funny, because Dewey is a terrible writer and is a very different [LAUGHS] pragmatist in some sort of sense, in terms of enquiry. And yet I think he's quite right that pragmatism is about *pragmata* and you need to be able to elicit the *pragmata*. So in a sense I'm just as interested in method and the social sciences as I am interested in metaphysics.

And do I have a metaphysics? No, I don't think I have a metaphysics, that's the problem. And the question of *experimental metaphysics*, which is a term I introduce in *Politics of Nature,* is a very important thing to believe. It's *experimental*, because if we have to begin to agree about the furniture of the world (are the objects held up by an inner kernel or connected? do we touch the object or not?) then politics is certainly finished, because there is actually no way we will settle these questions.

The second set of disputes (not disputes but of course I am much more critical of myself than you are of me) is because I take *Irreductions* to be a flawed, a completely flawed philosophy. And this is actually because of a point you mentioned very well, which is the virtuality question. So...

Graham Harman

Vir...?

Bruno Latour

The virtuality, the question of potentiality. So, this is slightly embarrassing but in fact three years after writing and publishing *Irreductions*, I embarked on another project which is completely parallel and absolutely antithetical to it. A project which has in mind metaphysics in that sense, which is the study of modes of existence or regimes of enunciation. So if I had to do a ... [PAUSE], if I had to do a book... No, this is silly, if I had to write a book on myself I would be much more critical. In one of the questions [submitted by participants before the conference] the translator of Tarde, [Alberto] Toscano, makes a very nice point, I think, that the whole of *Irreductions* supposes. "Actualism" is the word we can agree to use for it. Suppose that there is a unified metrics of force. So as you very nicely show, it has the effect of first solving the problem of human-nonhuman opposition, and then it has the nice polemical effect of marking the difference between *potentia* and force. "To *potentia*, to force, we will add nothing." And I still think it's useful because of the divide between might and right in the whole politics of epistemology which is often being studied now. That's basically done, okay. But it's done at a price. And the price is that the proliferation and the deployment of networks are uniformly grey. So, I would be much less favorable than you are toward this philosophy [in *Irreductions*]. I think it's a useful first step. But I think it's running into all the difficulties you mentioned, and maybe this is why it doesn't foot the bill for all the problems you raise at the end: an infinite regress, etc. I think it has many more difficulties than that. But the main difficulty is that it's a sort of generalized Nietzscheanism, which has the same weakness as Nietzscheanism but it is without defense against a seesaw, drifting into either vitalism in one hand, or a generalized power struggle on the other hand. It is defenseless against this accusation.

So this is why from the beginning, which is now twenty years ago, I tried to do something else entirely, which is much more sad for me. I'm speaking of the serious philosophical work which does connect with all of the figures you mention (still not very much with Heidegger, to my sorrow, but a lot with Whitehead and Hume and all the big guys) which is to add to the notion of network the *key* in which things are sent, so to speak. And what is obvious in *Irreductions*, which is a big weakness of actualism and what the concept of networks never managed to capture, is the notion of trajectory. So how many trajectories do we have? Can we trace the trajectory through different media? That's what I'm really interested in. Basically, can we shift from a theory of networks to a theory of modes of existence? And then I think we can tackle one of the very interesting questions in your book (which is a book about your own philosophy, not about my philosophy necessarily, and I don't necessarily want to have a philosophy anyway) which is the question of the continuation in time of the inanimate. Because I think there is a large literature now that once again tackles these big and really interesting questions that you mention at the end about cosmology. Where is the question of continuation, in other words, if a big question of occasionalism is: why do things subsist? Once [enduring] substance has been excluded, subsistence comes to the fore, and then the big question is how many ways there are for entities to graze their subsistence in the green pastures. And this is a metaphysical question, unabashedly so and I'm perfectly happy with that. But it's a very, very different question from the general theory of the way objects relate to one another. Because it's too different when you are a rock or when you are a creature from fiction or when you are a scientific reference and so on. And the differences here are much too strong, so that a sort of general features of what would be answering into relation no matter what you are, seems to me too much. I mean, you can think about it, but it is precisely the limit of *Irreductions*, which was good mostly for polemical reasons. But as you say very nicely somewhere, if a philosophy is only good because it's a critique of another philosophy, then it's not very good. And in that respect I think that *Irreductions* was in some sense a critique.

So, we agree of course on many things, but in a way I'm more interested in Graham's philosophy than in my philosophy. And Graham's philosophy has this very energetic way of pointing at the singularity and the materiality of beings. Then it has this very obsessive quest for an inner kernel which is different from its relations. And here I don't understand your point because I think we share exactly the same argument, and for me translation is necessary precisely because of the irreducibility of a singularity. And then we have two completely different ways of practicing our philosophical duties: one of them is yours, with much more seriousness than I can do of course, to know the classic works and see how they fit together, but with the difficulty for me that you then send the task of solving the details to the other professions. And I am interested in both; I am interested in a binary weapon. In the book on the Conseil d'État [*The Making of Law*] I'm exactly as interested in looking at every little way in which people speak or sit at the table as I am in understanding the essence of law in its most Socratic definition [LAUGHS]. So if there is a philosophical style which I can call mine, which I doubt very much, that would be what I'm really after. Why? Because if substance is excluded as the way to experience existence, then how many ways are there to subsist? That is what I am interested in.

And I'll finish with one last line (because I want to leave time for discussion) on one thing you don't speak about at all. It's Darwin! I'm a Darwinian. (Maybe it's the Tardean influence on me.) Here I can say that with great pride, because being a Darwinian at the LSE is a great advantage ... Not in the sense of Mrs. ...What's her name? The lady at the [INAUDIBLE]... Eh, what's her name? [INAUDIBLE] [LAUGHS] But Darwin in the sense of the secularization of singularity. Darwin is still... social Darwinism was registered even before Darwin died, but the task of registering the full secularization of differences [LAUGHS] without immediately (as you say very nicely) transforming it into a sort of *élan vital*, is still fresh. Darwin is still fresh. And in some very bizarre sense I'd like to be a Darwinian philosopher for whom the multiplicity of entities is actually set free. Now, is this the time when we answer the questions?

Edgar Whitley
I think...

Bruno Latour
No.

Edgar Whitley
...Graham will respond and then we will go to questions.

Graham Harman
I'll pick out a few things from this...

Bruno Latour
Just one last thing. Cosmologically, I entirely share your view about the fact that big questions have been abandoned. I don't believe they will be solved by philosophy but I believe they have to be tackled by politics. So, I wouldn't say the big questions are cosmological questions, but rather cosmopolitical questions. And the cosmopolitical question for me is the heart of what I am doing actually. I am more of a political philosopher in a way than a metaphysician– even though I am terrible in political philosophy, but that's another matter [LAUGHTER].

Graham Harman
I don't know if my notes are in very good order, so I'll pick out points as they occur to me. First of all, you certainly do have a metaphysics. *Irreductions* is about as compact a metaphysical

treatise as I've ever seen. And by the way, that does not mean I'm saying that that's the metaphysics and then you are just "applying" it to specific empirical cases. I would never be so arrogant as to say that this is the role of metaphysics. In fact I would make the same sort of Tardean point that you made last night, which is that there is no real difference in size between metaphysics and the various other disciplines. I am just linking things together in a different way. And so in a way it isn't fair to suggest that I'm trying to abstract some "meta" level that is not contaminated by the things. Those are simply the sorts of actors I work with. And I don't think they are incompatible with politics, by the way. I don't see why you say that, because I'm not claiming that "I have the final answer here and there is no room for further discussion." I am too much of a Heideggerian to say that. There are still going to be aspects of the things that I am not able to grasp. And conversation is needed to help negotiate... So I don't think the two procedures are necessarily in conflict. I don't think metaphysics necessarily renders politics in your sense impossible. On the contrary.

At the same time, I am not sure that you are simply following the cases and trying to get your metaphysics out of the cases, because pretty clearly the idea that things cannot be reduced was one of your guiding principles from very early on. And this obviously affects how you read Pasteur and the other cases. And that's not really a principle that was drawn from empirical observation, right? Maybe it was a principle that was drawn from your disgust and fatigue with all the attempts to reduce, which are perhaps not fruitful any more. But I think one of the principles that governs the way you look at cases is the idea that alliances are more important than hidden individual essences and potentialities. I'm glad you like the part in the book about occasionalism, very glad.

And you didn't say anything about Bergson today, but the last time I checked with you about this, you agreed that there is a difference between the two of you. Okay. Because I think this tendency to mix Latour, Whitehead, Bergson, Deleuze is very harmful. It's far too sloppy. So I am glad that you are on board with that claim. As for Darwin, I didn't mention him in the book simply because I wasn't trying to talk about all of your historical influences. That's what I had planned to do when working on that other book, the "School X" book, where I was trying to talk about all your other rivals and allies and colleagues. And you were emphasizing that Darwin ought to be part of that project, and I agreed. This project spun off from that one because it was simply becoming too long. That whole thing was going to be 900 pages or something and nobody was going to publish it, so this is a spin-off. Eventually I hope to go back and finish the other one that has Bergson and Whitehead and some of these other people in it, and there will be some Darwin in there at your request. We might need to have another conservation about that so I grasp it completely, but I can already see what you're up to there.

I am not sure that I understand your new book yet. I understand that you view it as an alternative system to *Irreductions*. And incidentally I made the joke in Cerisy[37] last summer that Bruno Latour is the only philosopher in history to have gone through his early and late phases simultaneously [LAUGHTER]. He has been publishing the earlier Latour all along, but all the while he's been working on the late Latour in the second manuscript, "The Modes of Existence," that we had the privilege to read this summer in Cerisy and which I hope will be published soon. You are going to work on it some more? Yeah, okay. Where there are actually different types, fourteen different modes of existence... right?

Bruno Latour
Yeah.

Graham Harman
Fourteen different modes in which the things can link with each other.

Bruno Latour
Now that's metaphysics, I agree [LAUGHS].

Graham Harman
I agree, that book is metaphysics, I just don't understand it. It's fascinating, but I don't quite get it yet. And you also say that the fourteen are determined empirically, they are not based on a philosophical structure of...

Bruno Latour
Empirically, yeah, sort of.

Graham Harman
... four groups of three, with two unifying, and that was how I was trying to read them. But no, you want to say that fourteen modes are drawn empirically from the history of Europe. Okay, so I'll wait until that book is out before I write a sequel to this commentary, about Latour's next book.

Bruno Latour
Can you explain, can you answer a question about ... because I still don't understand...

Graham Harman
About what?

Bruno Latour
I'd like people to share our misunderstanding about your point that I would be interested only in objects and their relations to the detriment of a singularity of the object?

Graham Harman
No, I think objects and relations are what you do work on. It's just a question of how you define objects and how you define relations.

The only problem with relations was the question of infinite regress. We need a medium where things are *directly* in contact, otherwise things are going to be separate forever unless we bring in God or the human mind to solve it, which we can't. So there has to be a place where direct contact does happen, otherwise we just get mediators between mediators between mediators, and never get to where the contact actually happens. The root problem we've always had is the Heideggerian theme I always bring in, about a thing not having anything to do with its relations. But this is actually the most important thing you've said just now. You seem to be saying that your view that things need to be translated already covers you on that front, and that the thing is already inexhaustible.

Bruno Latour
No, you said it very nicely…

Graham Harman
Okay.

Bruno Latour
…and I learnt it. [LAUGHTER] I didn't know I believed it until you said it [in the book]. [LAUGHTER]

Graham Harman
And I forgot that I said it [LAUGHTER].

Bruno Latour
Is that the end? That's what I said. [LAUGHTER]

Graham Harman
And I forgot that I said it until you mentioned it just now. [LAUGHTER] We'd better just keep learning from each other well into old age. Yes, that is true, you are someone who makes translations so necessary that things are inexhaustible. But in what does

that inexhaustibility consist? What is in the thing other than their relations with other things? It's kind of like Whitehead. For Whitehead too, the prehension is always going to be an oversimplification. But what the actual entity really is, is its past prehensions of all other things, right? There is no inner reality of an actual entity for Whitehead that exists apart from any of its prehensions. It's constituted by those prehensions, and then it just kind of has to move on to the next set of prehensions. It has to oversimplify the other entities and their past states. And so... yes, you are never going to exhaust the thing when you translate it but what is that thing that's being translated? It starts off as merely relational. It starts off as constituted only by its relations with other things. You say this yourself, in your point that I play with in the mock Socratic dialogue in the book, when you say that an entity is nothing more than its perturbations, transformations and modifications of an entity. That is what I am talking about. I would say that the thing is not just its perturbations, transformations and modifications of other entities. It is something beyond that, something over and above: one of your own favorite phrases. It's something more, over and above and beyond those relations and perturbations. And yes, this is the Heideggerian element in my work that we've never agreed about. We've argued about it for many years. I'm happy to open it up for questions unless you wanted to respond?

Bruno Latour

No, I wanted to answer, but I don't know when, to the questions which were sent in [by audience members]...

Edgar Whitley

Okay, if you are both happy we can open the floor to questions. It sounds like you want to respond, Bruno, to a couple in particular and then open up?

Bruno Latour
No, I don't know when this is. I think there is a moment in the agenda when we discuss what I have been sent by email? I don't know.

Edgar Whitley
Yeah, that's what we move to.

Peter Erdélyi
Yes, some of the participants have... submitted questions which we were considering for the panel discussion...

Bruno Latour
Oh, okay.

Peter Erdélyi
... later on but if some of those issues come up now as part of the natural discussion, that's fine.

Edgar Whitley
We now open it up to comments and questions.

Bruno Latour
Just one point about this, since we are discussing another book that has not been distributed as generously as yours, is that in this new book of mine about modes of existence, irreduction is one of the modes of existence. So it's one way of approaching the question, but one that is very important precisely because it does not accept the divide between might and right. But it has the limitation of being just one mode of existence, which is the deployment of actor-networks, so to speak. Just so that we are not unfair in the discussion [LAUGHS].

Graham Harman

Maybe I will address Aleksi [Aaltonen's] question first because it deals directly with something I forgot to answer: Bruno's point about pragmatism as a method versus philosophy's "furniture of the universe".

Bruno Latour

Oh yes, yes.

Graham Harman

I do think metaphysics gives the furniture of the universe. But that doesn't mean I think that it can do so absolutely and in final form. I was actually surprised to hear you say that you didn't mean the point about the microbes not pre-existing Pasteur in a literal, metaphysical sense. You just meant it as a kind of probe? Or as a kind of...? Because it certainly seems like you mean it seriously when you say that microbes did not exist before Pasteur discovered them. The other thing you said that's controversial, in a different place, is that you can't say Ramses II had tuberculosis, that this is an anachronism because tuberculosis [was not yet discovered] in ancient Egypt.

Bruno Latour

Another thing that got me into trouble [LAUGHTER].

Graham Harman

Do I understand now that you don't actually mean these things literally? That you mean it...?

Bruno Latour

No, no, I mean them literally, but the proof of a case has to be found *ad hoc*, in the actual occasion. They cannot be made into a general statement, because then they become uninteresting or too flippant.

Graham Harman

Right. I'm not sure I get that, but let me respond to Aleksi's question which is: "Is it possible that there could be both methodological and metaphysical readings of this controversy?" And I have only a slight idea about this that I came up with just yesterday, which is that maybe methods are better if they are wrong. In a sense, a method should be an exaggeration, shouldn't it? Methods are in some sense more powerful if they are metaphysically wrong. I thought of a few examples yesterday. One of them might be saying that everything is really just its relations. Why? Because that can get us to focus on the relations between things, and that does a lot of work for us. Instead of getting lost in all these speculations about what the inherent essence of the thing is, it can be useful to say "let's assume that the thing is only its relations." I've thought of other examples of this. One of them would be *Realpolitik*, I don't...

Bruno Latour

What?

Graham Harman

Realpolitik. I don't actually believe that everything nations do is governed by a cold calculation of national interest, but I do occasionally find it very refreshing to read [Henry] Kissinger and — what's his mentor's name? The guy that wrote *Politics Among Nations*... I don't remember that guy's name [Hans Morgenthau]... It can be very refreshing to read geopolitics as if all that's governing the decisions is cold national interest. It allows you to get rid of a lot of hypocrisies and moralisms that might otherwise cloud your vision. I don't think that's the full picture but I think it's a nice cold shower sometimes, as a very extreme method. The "hyperbolic" method I use in the book is another example of an extreme false method. You can actually do more justice to an author if instead of trying to find mistakes, you exaggerate it to the point where they've achieved total victory. We concede all of an author's points and then ask: "Where are we now? Has this solved all of our problems?" As opposed to the usual method of academic critique, which is to go around and poke holes and find twenty-eight mistakes in this author and thirty-one mistakes in that author. It doesn't really get us anywhere. So that's my idea about method: maybe method should be false, maybe that's when it's best.

Aleksi Aaltonen

I raised the question because it is something that every time you read Latour's books, this is something that people start arguing about. Microbes have to be somewhere before Pasteur made them existent, whereas for me it has been methodologically a quite nice insight that there was nothing to draw these things together before there was Pasteur who made them exist. I haven't been obviously thinking about it as a metaphysical question. So it has just been a nice methodological insight to look at the world. So maybe I am right that they don't have to be metaphysically correct to be useful in empirical research. Because first and foremost, I'm just a PhD student, so I'm interested in understanding what happens here in the empirical world.

Bruno Latour

But that is an important point because in spite of what Graham says, I am not sure I want to agree with him too fast about it. Because if metaphysics is interesting, *it is* as a method: as travel, as a way of getting at new insights. Actually I have noted the same sentence as you did with a question mark in Graham's manuscript because the opposition between pragmatism that works as a method and not as a metaphysics seems to me wrong in a way, because what is so interesting about pragmatism is basically because it allows you to go places. It is a trajectory, a way of doing things. So, a lot of the things I call philosophical are actually about how to go places. Why is it so difficult? I mean the principle of symmetry which I don't use so much now but which appears in another question [from an audience member], was very useful for that. You are dealing with science and technology and people are just stuck. Is it a philosophical point? Yes, but I would not put so much weight on the philosophy part, saying that humans and nonhumans are associated together. But as a trajectory toward getting at data, it has been extremely fecund. It is not an opposition between doing philosophy and doing social sciences, but an opposition between doing bad science and good science. That's the only thing which is of interest. And if it's metaphysics that goes there, then let's do metaphysics. If it is reading Heidegger which gets us there, then let's read Heidegger. If it's reading Garfinkel, let's read Garfinkel. The important thing is to get there.

And metaphysics asks at all of these different points that go to the heart of where the substance and the meat really are. I mean, in the case of a topic such as backward causation, the meat is this: as long as the difference between discovery and invention is not decided, you always go back to the classical distinction between the history of science on the one hand and the rest of history on the other. There is absolutely no way to get out. Then someone has to go there and tackle, in as much detail as possible, the question of extracting the backward causation from a specific case. Then after we can say that since it has been shown in one case, it is probably true in the other, and then we have the problem of generalization. But for me pragmatism and metaphysics should be connected very, very, very closely.

Graham Harman

Pragmatism is an interesting example of my point because what's the basic tenet of pragmatist method? It would be that if a dispute makes no practical difference, then it's not a real conflict, not a real dispute. The problem is that you don't always know what's going to make a difference when you're having an actual dispute. In response to the case I was talking about with the mediators coming in between any two terms, a pragmatist could just say, "well, it makes no difference how Joliot links to the neutrons; who cares how he saw them, how he measured them?" Of course you could also open that question up too and study it, but the pragmatist would just say it doesn't really matter where the ultimate point of connection is between things. You can just keep on opening the black boxes as far as you want; you don't need to know the exact place where things communicate. But *that in itself* becomes a kind of metaphysics. It becomes a kind of human-centered metaphysics where you say that all that matters is practical effects. And so it is not neutral on metaphysics as it claims to be. You either think that there is a reality outside of human experience or you don't. And if you do think so, then pragmatism can't be the method; you also have to be able to talk about things that don't make a practical difference to humans.

Bruno Latour
But pragmatism is not about practice, pragmatism is about *pragmata*, about objects. It is an experimentally-based philosophy. And in that sense I think here you are not employing your usual generosity with pragmatism because it is precisely the notion of "experimental" that is very important. So in the case you mention, the question which the pragmatists should tackle is: "Is there a protocol for an experiment in which Joliot's eyeball counts, or not?" But this is not the same as the question of practice. I think that's unfair to pragmatism.

Graham Harman
All right, it may be about *pragmata*, but it depends on how you define *pragmata*. If you define *pragmata* only in terms of their relations with other things, then that is a metaphysical presupposition too. By contrast, I am trying to say that the things are beyond those relations, and I don't think you need a protocol to say what...

Bruno Latour

It's because things are beyond relations that they have relations.

Graham Harman

That's my position, yes.

Bruno Latour

So, this is why I have never understood the opposition between having relations and being beyond relations because I mean every geographer will tell you that. If there is a road between two cities, it's because these two cities are not the same cities. So if the two cities were the same city, there would not be any road between them. It's because they are irreducibly two cities that we need a road between them. [LAUGHTER]

Graham Harman

That's right, but then the question is this: what are the cities themselves without the roads? Are you going to define them in terms of other relations to other cities or are you going to define them...

Bruno Latour

I mean, all of the geographers have worked on this question... Nigel [Thrift] has written a whole book about this question of cities...

Nigel Thrift

I apologize immediately. [LAUGHTER]

Bruno Latour

Actually, you must have written three books [LAUGHTER] (Nigel writes books in salvoes [LAUGHTER]) but of course the fact of having a road would have modified them. But the whole position between having relations and being beyond relations escapes me even now. I simply don't understand because it is precisely… If you mean this, this silly argument (and here I agree entirely with you) that if you make a sum of *qualia* and then you have a substance… I mean, who has actually ever said that? The Megarians?

Graham Harman

Most of the British Empiricists have said that. That substance is simply an arbitrary bundling of qualities.

Bruno Latour

Yes, but the beyond is always there. I mean that's even in Hume actually… But that's another question because the whole question of Hume is with the mind and habit and so on. And anyway the Brits are okay, let the Brits do their own thing [LAUGHTER]. But if the continentals or Europeans then… [LAUGHTER] It's funny because it is really something which is very powerful in your book. It's precisely the very, very powerful point that it's because things are irreducible that the relations have now center stage and that they are costly. And that every single one of them, whatever they do in terms of relations, they cannot escape and empty the powerful singularity. So you make the point, but then you seem to use it in opposition to what I say. And still I don't understand that.

Graham Harman

I'm sure we will come back to this later, maybe there is …

Edgar Whitley

Is that triggering any responses, further questions or clarifications that anybody wants to contribute?

Noortje Marres

Well, one brief point that you can maybe say a bit more about is the relations with agnosticism and pragmatism, the fact Graham that you find it very uninteresting to detect an object by its effects…?

Graham Harman

No, not uninteresting, just wrong. I think it is very interesting. [LAUGHTER]

Noortje Marres

Well, yeah, wrong. I think the crucial element there is the agnosticism that is built into the pragmatist method. So because pragmatists are not contemplative metaphysicians, because they say "we will not decide in advance what the world is made up of," this is why they go with this weak signal of the effect. Because that is the only way to get to a new object, an object that is not yet met nor defined. And that seems to be one of the important differences for this discussion as well.

Graham Harman

Except that Heidegger is also ultimately an agnostic, isn't he? I mean you are never going to know everything, everything is only going to be partially unveiled. So I think agnosticism is there too.

Noortje Marres

But that's different because he doesn't want to know. [LAUGHTER]

Bruno Latour

What do you mean, Noortje, that [William] James…? I mean in James, there are very, very beautiful words. James has a very nice way of answering, in spite of the fact that he is responsible for the metaphor that it's just practice, just for practical effect. He also has the vocabulary for a non-skeptical version of occasionalism. In your book there are two absolutely brilliant points which I hope you will develop in the last chapter (I am talking about Graham's book here). One is that the billiard balls, when they hit one another, have a very impoverished version of one another. Then you repeated that this morning, which is quite nice, that it doesn't take the human mind to have an impoverished version of the world, every entity [LAUGHS] has impoverished versions of the others as well. So that's a great moment. The other one, and it is connected to the agnosticism question, is that skepticism is an occasionalism. And what I sense in your objection is that pragmatism is actually a skeptical argument, a remnant of a skeptical argument. If there are only differences because there are effects, how do we know that it's not the way Joliot can hear that is really the important thing in making the connections. There is no literature on how to make sure of that.

Steve Woolgar always reminded me when we were doing *Laboratory Life*: why is the wastebasket not the most important thing to study in your laboratories, and why do you dismiss the wastebasket as unimportant? I did dismiss the wastebasket as uninteresting, and I think I had good grounds for that. But again in terms of skepticism there is no way [LAUGHS] you could dismiss the wastebasket as being the most important thing. So, James's solution is in the continuity of a connection, which is established. Again, it's a question of trajectory. So he answers the skeptics and he answers the "cash value" people, who were an inferior version of James, by this question of the continuity of a trajectory of learning, which for him is essential. And of course he made the unfortunate move of saying that this is as good as it gets. And of course then all of the metaphysicians jumped on him, saying that you are not ambitious enough, you just want an inferior version of it. But actually what he was trying to do is precisely to answer the skeptics. And it is the continuity of the trajectory of the production of proof which is so interesting in James, which I took up and expanded a bit in my industrial definition of truth conditions.

Graham Harman
Which I think is the most interesting passage in any of your books.

As for Joliot, I think you misunderstood my point about that. I am not trying to say that the problem is not being able to determine which is the most important mediation. I am trying to say that all the mediations have to be accounted for. Because as long as you have different entities, as long as you have any two entities linking with each other, there always needs to be a third entity mediating those. So I am not just saying there is no way to know whether it's Joliot and politics that's important or Joliot and the eardrum, I am saying that any two entities at all have to be accounted for in their relation and you can't keep inserting mediators in between two terms and passing the buck as to where the causation actually occurs. And so there has to be some third term as a medium. And I didn't talk about that in this book yet, I'm going to talk about it in the final chapter. I have a different solution; that's not so important today. But let's just express it in negative terms. I think you cannot keep on saying that there has to be a third term mediating any two others and not finally reach a point where the mediation stops and where there is a direct contact of some sort. Now that's paradoxical because your whole philosophy (wonderfully so) is about requiring mediators. But it can't go on forever; there has to be a point where contact happens. And what I worry about is that if we don't specify that point metaphysically, then it becomes just a kind of *ad hoc* practical decision, which of course is fine when writing history. You could say: "all right, it seems like the case of Joliot connecting politics and neutrons is interesting but Joliot and the eardrum is not that important, so we can stop there." And that's fine for purposes of writing history, but it is not fine for metaphysics.

Bruno Latour
Why?

Graham Harman
Why? Because you haven't explained how the contact occurred.

Bruno Latour

But metaphysics is not for explaining. It is the first principle of *Process and Reality*. Philosophy is not in the business of explaining anything. Actual occasions explain what happened, not philosophy. If there is one thing which philosophy should not do, it is to try to explain anything. That's where our disagreement is. Philosophy is not in the business of explaining. This is not at all the same thing. Philosophy is in the business of allowing the explanation to go far enough, to help the explainers to move in the explanatory trajectory but not to provide an explanation. What explanation would you add to my infamous statement about Pasteur and the microbes? Doing more archival work on Pasteur?

Graham Harman

No, you'd have to account somehow for what the reality of the thing was before it was discovered by anything else. What the interaction of the microbes is with other things in the environment that humans didn't know about yet. That's what you've got to do in the metaphysics to…

Bruno Latour

It isn't really, Graham. I mean I am sure that it isn't. Actual occasions have no other explanation than actual occasions, and philosophy is not in the business of explaining it. Because the metalanguage and the language are in a different situation on that. I think that's the problem with the student of information systems in my *Reassembling the Social* book. Graham wants a metalanguage that provides an explanation, and I disagree with that.

Graham Harman

I'm just trying to make sure that we're not getting too trapped in the word "explanation" here, as this is really a disagreement between us and not… This sounds suspiciously like the disagreement I had with Gerard de Vries in Amsterdam a few weeks ago when he said the same thing in response to my book: that philosophy is not about explaining. The problem when you say this, I think, is that you simply end up with a different kind of explanation. You end up saying that what constitutes reality is its importance for the person who is trying to go further in the explanation. That's a metaphysical decision, that's not an innocent methodological step, right? What you are saying is that it doesn't really matter, there isn't really anything outside of the person who is trying to find the explanation. It is a human-sounding philosophy, it is not realist enough for me.

Bruno Latour

No, I'm not saying that either. I agree with you about the objection you make. And I'm just here a strict Whiteheadian: actual occasion, that's my job. [PAUSE] But philosophy is not in the business of providing foundations for anything. Maybe there is a slight...

Graham Harman

Foundations? I'm not sure it's ...

Bruno Latour

Foundational.

Graham Harman

See, I don't think it's foundational, what I'm saying. Foundational to me would be if you claimed to give it some sort of enduring foundation that you're going to build everything on. I'm too Heideggerian to say that. I think the foundation is always going to be elusive. I think you are not trying to give it a foundation, you are trying to give it a reality that is outside of the relations. You are never going to know exactly what that reality is, and that's why it *can't* be a foundation. But it has to be there, because you can't account for the situation just with the relations. There has to be something doing the relating.

Edgar Whitley

OK, there is a question there, second, third, fourth.

Peter Hallward

I also have the same question for you Graham, so if you don't mind I'm going to ask it again. You argue that objects have a kind of inner essence which withdraws from and subsists in the absence of relations with other objects. How then do you understand the nature of objects whose essence, if they have one, seems to depend on the relational system to which they belong? Take a canonical example, a chess game: the game involves distinct objects or pieces. Their individuality, however, is a function of the relations that define the rules of chess. In what sense is a rook 'a rook' outside of these relations? Abstract the game of chess, and you have a piece of plastic which could itself enter into other kinds of relations. It seems to me this applies across the board: the object that is a building or a bridge is so only in a particular relational context, relative to certain kinds of human interaction and use, and so on. How about an apparently simpler case along the same lines: say that you look for a camping site, as a place to spend the night. You are involved then in a wide range of relations with a landscape and an itinerary, you ask yourself some basic questions: where am I going to pitch my tent, is there water nearby, is the ground dry and flat, etc. My question is: if you eliminate these relations and questions, if you eliminate the camper, are you left with an 'object' that you might still describe as a campsite? Will this object remain if a new set of relations comes to dominate that landscape? Would it retain an essence worthy of the name? If not, given the way you define objects, is there a problem?

Graham Harman

Okay. I want to talk about your first point which is that relations in many ways already solve the problem. Well, yes and no. Relations do occur, so in that sense the problem is solved by reality, yeah.

Things are not just placed in vacuum-sealed bubbles that never touch. They do touch. And that's what has to be explained. Given that an object by analysis reveals that it should be something that withdraws from all relations (at least by my analysis) then you just have to figure out that there is this paradox. Because, on the one hand, objects seem like they should be isolated, and yet relations and events do occur. And so what I am trying to do is account for how that happens. And I don't think it helps just to start by saying it is a *fait accompli* and we don't need to worry about it. That's like answering Bergson's charge that movement can't be made out of cinematic frames by showing a movie and saying: "look, the picture is moving, so Bergson is wrong." Well, yes, but that doesn't give an explanation of what movement is.

As far as the chess pieces, you asked this a year or two ago and I wasn't thinking about it as much as I should have but it just popped into my mind: saying that there is no rook-in-itself in a chess game is sort of like saying there is no I-in-myself if you are looking at my family structure, right, like my relation with my brothers and my parents. Yes, of course, if you look at that as a chess game... What a horrible metaphor for a family [LAUGHTER]... If you look at that as a system of relations between these five people, yes, then of course *qua* family member I make no sense in myself outside of that, but *qua* individual I do. Now with chess pieces it is a little less interesting because a rook in itself is not very interesting, it is a pretty impoverished … well, it has a certain physical structure, and some of them are quite pretty in some of the chess sets.

As far as the campsite, I'd say something similar. Yes, there is a campsite-in-itself, and the way you can see this is by counterfactual examples. You can be at a campsite and say: "wow, wouldn't such-and-such a person love this?" And you can sort of imagine in your mind how that person would react to this particular campsite. And what they would be hypothetically reacting to (if you consider that thought experiment) is not your reaction to it and his reaction to it and the reaction of everyone else who is there now. No, you are imaging their reaction *to the campsite*, which is something that by definition is not going to be commensurable with anyone else's reaction to the campsite. None of us have fully grasped what that campsite means. Other people can be imagined coming, different animals can be imagined set loose in the campsite that might react to it in different ways. And so I don't have a problem with saying there is a campsite-in-itself. Even if something is created only by relations like a campsite, like society (DeLanda talks about this in his new book [*A New Philosophy of Society*[38]])... humans *create* society and yet there is *still* a society-in-itself that we never fully grasp. So I don't see it as that difficult to think that there is an in-itself for everything that's created.

Bruno Latour
Things-in-themselves are actually things that you reach, which is always a paradox.

Graham Harman
What is?

Bruno Latour
Things-in-themselves are always the things that you actually reach, which is very funny in Kant. So it's like tourism. You always want to be alone, to go to a faraway place and then you resent having all these other tourists that are there [LAUGHTER] but actually the thing-in-itself is what you reach. So it is always a paradox, an epistemological version of the truth condition.

Michael Witmore
I wanted to ask Graham a little more about the word *metaphysics* because I think some of the debate that is emerging is about what the meaning of that word is. And let me say what I think your position is, Graham, and maybe you will tell us more about why

you want that version. But as I understand it, you're looking for a metaphysics that is not a foundation, that is mobile, that is capable of designating various ontological elements as being active and passive, of having agency in one moment and no agency the next. However, you are uninterested in a metaphysics that is so flat or so adherent to the punctuality of occasions, so trapped within it, that all one can say about those occasions is that they happened here, here, here, and here. In other words, you want to avoid a metaphysics whose practice would then be serial redescription of the nets in the mode of chronicle history. But you also want to avoid something like foundationalism. Does that seem like a fair representation of what you want to do with the word and maybe some of the problems you perceive of how the word might be misused?

Graham Harman

That's right. I agree with all of that; it was completely accurate. I would just add a few things to it. I guess there is still a basically Heideggerian strand in my work, and I don't think it is very easy to be a Heideggerian foundationalist. The foundation is always slipping away from you in his work, and he doesn't even call himself the last philosopher as every preceding great philosopher did. So no, it is not a foundation, I really do not think that we derive empirical facts from this foundation at all. I think we are inspired by empirical facts. I read mostly non-philosophical materials. When I go into bookstores I usually go away from the philosophy section; it's usually too boring. I find myself in any other subject (history, science) precisely because I am more inspired by these "mere empirical details," which is not what I really think they are. I can't quite account for why these have a greater philosophical influence on me than philosophy books these days, but they do. So I do think that individual cases are important, and yes, they shouldn't be trapped in punctual occasions. There is something outside those occasions that can't be grasped by them.

Maybe I should also clarify the difference between my use of the word *metaphysics* and the use of it by, say, Heidegger and Derrida, where it is pejorative. This might not be familiar to everyone here today. Metaphysics for Heidegger and Derrida is bad because it is "ontotheology." It means that you are taking one particular being and using it as the exemplar that explains the rest. And I think this is nicely attacked in Bruno's *Irreductions* as well. What they are attacking is simply a form of reductionism, saying that there cannot be any one entity that explains all other entities. And so no, I'm not hoping to revive that kind of metaphysics, which I think is rightfully dead.

For me metaphysics means something more like realism. That there is a reality that escapes any of its manifestations. You can never be sure quite what it is, but you can offer some description of what the structures of that reality are. It's not totally hopeless as Kant seems to think it is. I think that's what philosophy can do. Philosophy is just an attempt at… or metaphysics, at least, is an attempt to dig down a few feet further into the ground than people think you can. It is not to find the bedrock. I don't think we'd find that.

Bruno Latour

Can I ask a question of this gentleman?

Graham Harman

Yes.

Bruno Latour

What's wrong with serial redescription? Because in fact serial redescription would be a pretty good definition of what I would call metaphysics. If, of course, to *serial* and *redescription* you add… how would I put it, *punctual*? …Or the *key* with which they maintain their subsistence. And in that sense serial redescription seems to be a very good definition for the social sciences as well as for philosophy. We accompany the task of the entities in their survival, so to speak, and their maintaining their subsistence in a very, very practical manner.

Michael Witmore

I think I asked it that way because I also wanted to think of what your practice might be. So my next question would be: "What's the difference between the addition to serial redescription that you are keen on, versus the depth of metaphysical reflection that Graham's system has? What is the difference between the two?"

Bruno Latour

Well, it's better to be a serial redescriber than a serial killer. [LAUGHTER].

Graham Harman

I would agree with that too. [LAUGHTER] Serial redescription is what Bruno does. I think that is a good description to use. It is not a good description of what I do. So I think you hit on something important.

Bruno Latour

Oh, I love it. I am a serial redescriber. Now I know who I am. [LAUGHTER] Thank you very much.

Graham Harman

Well, in Michael's pre-submitted question [he] touched on this too. Is there a practical difference between the two? Yes. And the answer I thought of for this yesterday on the train is one that Bruno refuted somewhat last night in his very nice talk on Tarde. I was going to say that one thing that has always made me uncomfortable in Bruno's histories is a certain lack of sympathy for... not just for the losers, because people have criticized you for this before, that you overvalue the winners and give short shrift to the losers. I'd put it slightly differently. I don't mind that you give short shrift to the losers. What bothers me is that I think there's a difference between deserving and undeserving losers. And I think it is the undeserving losers that get lost in this philosophy. Bruno has no sympathy for the lonely neglected genius, a figure that doesn't really appear in his histories. If Pasteur fails at his translations, it's as good as if he never existed. Personally I wouldn't go that far. I think that, even without subscribing to some naive idea of latent genius in the person before they do what they do, it's not meaningless to look at some case and say: "what a tragedy, that person had a great idea and it just didn't catch on at the right time." Is that really a meaningless statement? I admit, in practical terms it turns out to have been a failed idea; it doesn't matter to anyone. But I think there is a difference between good and bad losers. It might not always be easy to judge which is which. But when we write counterfactual histories this is what we do, isn't it? We try to find things that could have happened, hidden strengths that were not tapped, possibilities that were there. We don't treat all those failed possibilities equally, do we? We know that some of them are more likely than others, more likely to have succeeded than others.

So I think maybe if you confine yourself to redescription, serial redescription, there is a possibility that you are too trapped at the level of what actually happens. Now, I don't know enough of the ANT literature to know how much has been done in a different direction, how many possible counterfactual cases have been done in the literature. Maybe a lot. But the reason I backed off from this complaint a bit last night is that Bruno did a nice job of showing that Tarde didn't necessarily deserve to lose [his intellectual battle with Durkheim for dominance over French sociology]. He lost after all, but there are all these riches in his sociology that Bruno was trying to bring back last night in the lecture and at dinner afterward, and he did so very eloquently. So obviously you are aware of this, I just think that there may be a little more room for the failed genius than he leaves in his philosophy.

Bruno Latour
But that would be philosophy of history. I am not sure I have any ideas about this. But serial redescription is a powerful way of following an institution, for instance. What is an organization actually, even in organization theory, even in the most classical sense in management, if not a serial redescription which starts again (and it's true) every morning. I didn't know that for sure but now that I am a head of a school I know [LAUGHTER] that it's actually literally true. And that the metaphor I used many years ago of baboons is a good word to describe an organization as big as Sciences Po [LAUGHTER], that you reinvent the organization every morning. It's exactly that: the lack of subsistence of it. So [LSE FIRE ALARM BELL STARTS RINGING] in occasionalism and in the punctuality of existence, the organization is a very trustworthy animal to study, because their way of maintaining their subsistence is visible and can be empirically studied in a dramatic manner that we might forget for these things or these sort of beings there [POINTS AT PLASTIC CUP]. But for a "moral person," as we say in French, a *person morale*, or a corporate body in English? For a corporate body it is extremely visible. So is not a *corporate body* a good case study for metaphysics? I think so.

Because one of the things which is always forgotten in the case of microbes is that there are billions of microbes. So it is actually an immense problem, what we mean by their pixelization. I now have a student who is studying yeast in a laboratory in the South of France. Yeast is always coming by the billions! There is a fridge. The whole laboratory turns out to be a fridge where yeast are taken in and out and they … everyone is troubled with it… That is where metaphysics is useful because these poor biologists are struggling with the impossible task of having completely artificial, completely natural swarms of yeast by the billions, that they have to qualify in the Kripkean sense of the rigid designator. And my metaphysics would be this… to understand the yeast we have to read Kripke, but of course it's the yeast which is interesting. Thank you very much for "serial redescriber" [LAUGHTER], a marvelous term...

Edgar Whitley

Lucas also has his own baboons to look after...

Lucas Introna

Yes, yes... One of the ways in which Bruno deals with this problem of "explanation" versus "description" is to use the term "explication." And explication is this unfolding. And in a way... if explication is this unfolding, then your unfolding is its own explanation, and that's achieved through the serial description, or redescription. But what I understand your criticism to say is: how do we know that the unfolding has been sufficient for the explication to have happened? In other words, what's the criterion for stopping? And in the Socratic dialogue with the student [in *Reassembling the Social*] Bruno has an answer. He says well, when you've done 50,000 words.

Bruno Latour

He is going to accuse me of pragmatism. [LAUGHTER] And that is perfectly [INAUDIBLE].

Lucas Introna

... and in a way that's yeah, a very pragmatic answer. But it seems to me that's problematic. Because coming back to your criticism, in a way the very next unfolding, the very next serial description, might invalidate or bring into question all descriptions that have gone before. And so how do we know that the next..., or the choice we made to describe A rather than B, to unfold A rather than B, that that choice might have in fact been fatal in the description. How do we know? And since we don't have any criteria, we can't make that choice beyond saying well, we've done 50,000 words. Or you know, "time's up, project's finished, can't go any further." And so I wondered whether that's a way of thematizing this difference between your need for some explanation, or rather explication, that is sufficient at some level and your pragmatic answer to 50,000 words.

Graham Harman
Except in this case I would also give the same advice to the student.

Lucas Introna
Sure. [LAUGHTER]

Graham Harman
I think pragmatism works as a method, even if it fails as a metaphysics. And with writing it is extremely important to say: okay, this book will be finished. I did that with this book, actually. I said: "this book will be finished when it's August 25 and I have to fly to Amsterdam ten hours later." And that's the point I reached rather than the last chapter, everything was structured according to that arbitrary deadline: how much can I fit into these few weeks? So pragmatism is a good way to write, but that doesn't mean it's… You see this as somehow bearing on the difference between these two approaches?

Lucas Introna
Why is that a sufficient criterion? So the question is, it might be that the choice you make in terms of describing A rather than B or stopping your description at this particular point, that that stopping might have been just prior to the explication that would have given a more adequate explanation or adequate explication.

Bruno Latour
Well, that's a failed experiment.

Lucas Introna
Okay [LAUGHS].

Bruno Latour

That's where I am a pragmatist in the good sense of the word, a pragmatist in the Deweyan sense. And now we're talking about serious social sciences for which there is no true protocol; there are no criteria in the sense that there is no scientific method. And actually Nancy Cartwright here in this School has written the funniest paper on scientific method ever, by taking the average advice from all the books about scientific method, and they are extreme banalities [LAUGHTER]. Something like "read the literature, listen to colleagues, don't listen too much to colleagues" [LAUGHTER] and "proceed with caution," I mean something which is completely absurd. Every criterion of where you stop the research and where you begin research is of the same banality. But now the setup of the experimental situation in which you yourself work, on your own work and your own thesis, is a crucial question which is exactly as difficult, as constraining, as it is in the natural sciences. Even more so because in the natural sciences a lot of things help you paradigmatically to decide where to focus.

So the big problem of the social sciences (and the same for philosophy) is to invent the experimental protocol which is adjusted to the specific recalcitrance of the beast you want to study. But the fact that there is no general principle doesn't mean that it's "everything goes." On the contrary, because there are no criteria, the constraints of a case are so important. But if they are pragmatic in the good sense, they have to adapt. What do you want to study? How much money do you have? And what is the beast you want to follow? And if it is studying a tribe in New Guinea, it is not the same equipment as if you want to study an organization or a yoghurt factory or an information system. So here I don't think there is any disagreement about this. The social sciences are obsessed by epistemological questioning in a way that no science, no real science is. You never have a chemistry class that starts with the methodology of chemistry; you start by doing chemistry. And the problem is that since the social sciences don't know what it is to be scientific, because they know nothing about the real sciences, they imagine that they have to be listing endless numbers of criteria and precautions before doing anything. And they usually miss precisely what is interesting in natural sciences which is [LAUGHS] a laboratory situation and the experimental protocol!

But this is what I tried to explain to the student in the book. In our field, it means writing. Writing is our protocol and writing is our laboratory, and it's as difficult to set up good writing as it is to set up a good laboratory. I don't think that's what I'm questioning here, because I had the privilege of seeing some of the students of Graham in Cairo, and probably here we don't disagree at all on how to direct them [BOTH LAUGH].

Graham Harman
Yes.

Bruno Latour
That's not a metaphysical opposition, it's just the way to get rid of epistemology. But it is a detoxification cure that has to be taken repeatedly, because epistemology always creeps back in.

Peter Erdélyi
I'd like to deploy this experimental apparatus that Professor Latour had alluded to earlier, the Heidegger-Latour situation here. One of the points that Graham appears to be making is that for Heidegger there is this withdrawn realm that's inaccessible and which has been demonstrated through this present-at-hand and ready-to-hand dualism that he has developed. In *Reassembling the Social* on the other hand, practically the whole book starts to point to this final chapter where it is promised that we will behold something through this new topology that you develop. And there we encounter the image of the plasma, which is said not to be inaccessible but is something that is unknown. It is not hidden, but is unknown. And actually I don't want to pre-empt Isabelle

[Doucet]'s question, since she has also asked a question about plasma. But I would be curious to see, what is the role of plasma? Or is it perhaps a metaphysical discovery of the *Reassembling the Social* experiment?

Bruno Latour

Well, we'll talk again because I think there is another question on plasma, right?

Edgar Whitley

Yeah.

Bruno Latour

But, this is an ANTHEM point. And even though my knowledge of Heidegger is not as strong of course, Graham reminded us that he was a student of Husserl. So Heidegger has to do a lot of work to keep his own turf out of the great grasp of the natural sciences. These guys (Husserl is the same) are obsessed by the domination of the natural sciences. And one of the points by Graham, which is very nice in his book, is that we are not obsessed by this question. And we don't want to leave naturalism to the enemy either. And when I say we, I mean science studies, which is really my home. And that is a very big difference. So plasma is what appears once the so-called natural sciences are added to the pot, so to speak, and made to circulate, not to cover the whole. See, you have to realize that these guys in the nineteenth century... almost all the way until the ecological crisis really started to modify the situation in the 1980s, they had to struggle to get just a little bit of space which was not invaded by the natural sciences, biology, economics, and information systems [LAUGHTER]. They had to have a little plot where they could cultivate their little carrots and cabbages. If not, it would be taken out, exactly like you still have to fight here just to exist against the Dawkinses and all these other guys here in this world. I mean, Darwin has disappeared basically...

So, what people don't understand is that when you do science studies you have completely different views of all that. The whole space is actually empty. And then in this very, very empty space where ignorance is the rule basically, you have circulating in the full vein, the very, very, very full vein, which is the circulation of active and formatted knowledge about mathematics, and about chemistry, and about physics, and about sociology, and about economics. So it is a reversal of background and foreground. Plasma is what you do when, to your shock, you make all of the formatted knowledge circulate inside the landscape. And when you don't accept the situation which has been the situation of our predecessors (I am not talking about the Middle Ages, because someone asked a question about it, which is much more interesting than that) but the modernist predicament is largely that you left the primary condition to the enemy, so to speak. And then of course you suffocate and then you try to get just a little bit of things. And we have to find it in precisely this very, very pious style of Heidegger. But we are now on a completely different landscape.

Now, how do you call what is not formatted plasma? I mean, you can abandon the word if you want. But I think that's the point with our criticisms: we are never in awe of or in dispute with the natural sciences. We like them because they occupy so little space! And when you're struck by the ecological crisis, immediately you recognize a completely different territory. Here we know barely anything; we are in a state of complete ignorance. And then you have this very, very small channel of knowledge in the middle of a completely empty space. So suddenly you breathe (lots of space!) but then you are terrified by our shared ignorance, and then the question of reassembling the collective becomes central. I think that's the difference, in terms of landscape, between us and the Husserls. They had to struggle to survive. In Graham's book on Heidegger,[39] there is a very nice passage on Husserl's situation, and it was a matter of survival. How can we survive the natural sciences? Now I start with the question: "how can we ally ourselves with the natural sciences to survive?" The whole landscape is literally different now that the earth has taken political center stage.

Nikiforos Panourgias

Just following up from Peter… Maybe what Peter was trying to ask is: what is this unformatted knowledge? How are we supposed to get hold of it, to consider it?

Bruno Latour

Oh, it's extremely easy. These are the missing masses of all the formatted version of: what is management, what is an organization, what is an interchange, what is a religion, what is a science? You delineate it. If you do, the easiest way to do it for Westerners is to do a little exercise of description. I did that when I was here. You do a one-page, 3000 [millimeter] size description… this looks really simple but… [SHOWS PAPER WITH NOTES] and immediately you dip into the non-formatted plasma. You could not achieve even one formatted situation without relying on the plasma, actually. So it is a very strange situation because (I think I have used this metaphor before) if all of knowledge is the subway, then all the blanks in the subway is the plasma. But of course the blanks are the genuine reality. They are what feed the rest, allows them to work.

So if you take an organization (I'm very obsessed by the question of organization now). No organization would work one minute if it were not constantly drawing on this reserve of… so-called unformatted plasma. The point is just that we don't know what it is exactly, of course. And every single organizational theorist immediately has to draw a diagram… I mean, every generation changes, but it shows *informal connection, interaction*… Every management consultant has to invent one of these just because it's like buckets taken out of a plasma, so to speak, to fill in and make the machine work; if not the machine would just stop. And then if you take formalism... I have just published an article in *Social Studies of Science*[40] on a fabulous book by Reviel Netz[41] on Greek geometry. But plasma is everywhere. To obtain the formatting of the mathematical demonstration in Greece, you need a non-formal description. What is a non-formal description of formalism if not the drawing of the plasma in order to obtain the effect of the demonstration? Which was of course missed when people had to fight formalism because formalism was supposed to occupy the whole landscape. And if you have the formal description of formalism, then the problem of course disappears. The whole landscape is occupied by formalism. But if you have a non-formal description of formalism, then the big question is: how do you obtain formalism for even one minute? Well, by drawing on non-formal masses, etc. etc. So, plasma is completely... I mean it is a concept. If you want to show where the plasma is, I say everywhere because it is... it's not the unformatted that's the difficulty here. It's what is in between the formatting. Maybe this is not a very good metaphor. But it's a very, very different landscape, once the background and foreground have been reversed and the sciences have been added to the landscape, instead of being what defined the landscape.

Another philosopher who is very interesting is Peter Sloterdijk, because he has a completely different set of metaphors for that. And that would be the outside of spheres in Sloterdijk's vocabulary. You survive if you are in the air-conditioning of the sphere. Well of course, but when you are in the air-conditioning you don't see what makes the air-conditioning work. And that would be... you wouldn't call it plasma but it would be the same concept, what allows for the sustenance of a very small pocket of existence in which we are. And again, even more forcefully in Sloterdijk than in myself, the ecological crisis is the thing that eats at philosophy in an interesting way, so to speak.

Graham Harman

The really surprising thing about the plasma was how large you said it was. Like the whole of London, whereas the networks would merely be the size of the London Underground. That was very striking for those who think that your entire world is made up of networks. There is such a vast mass outside of it.

Edgar Whitley

Very quickly…

Catelijne Coopmans

I just wanted to go back to your discussion about empirical cases and the importance of them in relation to metaphysics. And I wonder if it makes sense to say that the actors that populate these cases actually do metaphysics themselves. So their relating can produce a distinction between surface and depth, for example. And if that is the case, does it matter for either the practice of social science or metaphysics?

Graham Harman

Objects doing their own metaphysics: I like that phrase. [PAUSE] I'm not sure what to do with it. I have been working so hard not to have myself called a panpsychist because everybody assumes that if I am talking about objects that relate to each other then I must be saying that objects have minds. And I have been trying so hard to ward that off, and I am going to have to try to settle this issue once and for all fairly soon. But nonetheless, I'm still drawn to this image of objects doing metaphysics even if I don't want to say they have minds. Inside, I feel torn in two directions on this question. Can you give an example of objects producing their own distinctions between surface and depth? I don't doubt that there are millions but… do you have one in mind?

Catelijne Coopmans

I've been working on this study about medical imaging and how medical images get digitized... I am trying to make the argument that in the course of that action of digitizing and presenting the digital version of a medical image, particular distinctions between surface and depth emerge from the relations that are enacted in that situation. So thinking about that case, what I am interested in is: would it be possible to say that there are new foundations, new fundamentals being produced by the actors in the situation?

Bruno Latour

I think that's an important point, because that's where I am worried by the fact that if you stabilize this question, which is the relation... I mean, what is really important for Graham, which is the connecting. Do actors, do entities touch? Do they need to touch one another? If you have to stabilize this vocabulary, you might miss the metaphysics produced by a new entity which is very powerful in digital imaging. It is a completely new, different way in which background and foreground or pixels and wholes are connected. And that would be a worry. Just to give you one very simple example of which I am very proud. Through my ideas, I have managed to have the greatest painting in the Louvre, sixty-seven square meters in size, robbed from the Louvre, facsimiled and transported back to the original place in Venice without being touched.[42] And the Louvre has not discovered the robbery; it is very funny [LAUGHTER]. Full digital technology... We actually managed a second original which is even more perfect than the first, because it's actually better and it's back in its original place.

Now, here is a typical case where the whole metaphysical apparatus had to be mobilized, from Benjamin's definition of what is an original, what is a copy, what is a subsistence, the whole question of dispute between the original and the copy. The result is that this work by the great artist Adam Lowe first had the Venetians in tears when they saw what they believed was a mere facsimile, and what we argued was the second original. Then we realized that the aura of a painting in the Louvre had been robbed. And actually now, if you go to Venice, you will notice that for the first time, not for the older people here but for the younger, where you see a very great masterpiece without being blocked by endless security guards and so on, is now the *Nozze di Cana* of Veronese in Venice. Not in the Louvre! In the Louvre it's in the Mona Lisa Room. It is surrounded by guards. You can't see it because it is so big that actually you bump into the Mona Lisa [LAUGHTER], into the Japanese looking at the Mona Lisa, you cannot see the painting. But when you are in Venice, since it's a facsimile, it cost... I mean, it is not even protected. There is no air-conditioning, there is no guard. You are alone for the first time with a major work of art. Okay, that's the sort of case where for me the whole question of metaphysics —about what it is to reproduce, what it is to do a facsimile, what is an original, what is a digital technique— are being transported anew and offered for study to people like us.

And that's where the positioning of metaphysics might be different. Here it's crucial not to make assumptions about the basic furniture of *original* and *reproduction*, because as you mentioned, the digital technology modified entirely, locally, what it is to reproduce something and what it is to reproduce. I asked the guys in the Louvre: you didn't even notice that your painting has been robbed? [LAUGHTER] This is very odd. People go to Venice and now they are flocking to the Fondazione Cini to see a real Veronese. It is at the place for which Palladio meant it. So that's practical... that's empirical metaphysics for me.

Graham Harman

I have no good answer to that, it was a dazzling story but...

Edgar Whitley

That does give us a good time to break for lunch.

[Lunch]

Edgar Whitley

I'm happy for conversations to continue… There were certainly plenty of lively conversations over lunch. But from the fact that you have chosen to come back to the room I am assuming you also have some interest in hearing the panelists. So we have Graham and Bruno remaining at the front to take some of the questions. But we are joined also by Lucas Introna who is Professor of Organisation, Technology and Ethics and currently Head of Department…

Lucas Introna

For my sins…

Edgar Whitley

…for his sins, at Lancaster University Management School and Noortje Marres who is Marie Curie Research Fellow at the Centre for Study of Invention and Social Process and Sociology at Goldsmiths. I think over lunch we decided that you would have some thoughts and some comments with which to start. We also have the various questions that people submitted, some of which have not yet been covered and perhaps we want to come back to. And of course Graham and Bruno also have an opportunity to contribute as well. We are nominally going till about 1:30, and we do want to try to finish by about 2 o'clock in total. So if we extend this discussion, then closing statements might need to be a little bit shorter. Over to you.

Noortje Marres

Well, our job description as panelists included two items: one was to take a position, and another was to try to summarize or explicate, amplify some of the points that had arisen in the morning. So what I'd like to do first, is speak briefly for a couple of minutes about this central question of the experimental metaphysics which I think…

well, I'd like to say something about that, and then summarize three points which I think are all crucial, either points of contention or perhaps more productively points to grapple with and struggle with.

On the point of experimental metaphysics, I feel that I need to stand up for actor-network theory a bit, in the sense that there is one aspect of actor-network theory which I think is a very important challenge to metaphysics or intervention in metaphysics that maybe hasn't received so much attention. And that is the point that actor-network theory developed a particular style of doing event-thinking. And because Graham says, "well, all this process philosophy business. I'm glad to keep Latour or actor-network theory in a different camp," it is something that I think doesn't always come out. And maybe the fact of Latour himself trying to shift metaphysics to a different terrain, that of the modes of existence, has also made me take an interest again in this question of the "event" aspect of earlier actor-network theory. And why do I think that it is important? On the one hand, I think it's important for the simple reason that by focusing on actors as events and by studying translation as an event —which is something that Graham does state explicitly in his book— by doing that, actor-network theory actually pushes process philosophy, I think, and also event-thinking in a particular way. And what actor-network theory adds to that perspective is that it realizes that, as soon as we say that we are not going to address the question of what is, but we are instead going to take as our starting point stuff that is happening, as soon as you make that shift, in a sense you suspend ontology. So the point of the flat ontology, the point of the symmetry between humans and non-humans, is also that actor-network theory presents a way of undoing ontology. And I do think that Graham is right to say yes, but to really make use of ANT we have to reconstitute an ontology, or perhaps its ontology, but I think this undoing of it is absolutely crucial for two reasons.

One question that is relevant here is: why does ANT need to

undo ontology and say "we start with these blobs of humans and non-humans as an amorphous field, completely inelegant and inarticulate?" It is because they are studying change. They are studying change in a technological society: that is what I understand actor-network theory to be about. It's about saying that we have a world where continuously new entities are added to the range of existing entities, everything continuously changes and yet in this modern technological world everything stays the same. We have these stabilized regimes. We have these black boxes that aren't possible to open. How is it possible for both of these things to be the case? And this means that to address that question, you then have to look at how ontologies are articulated in events or in practice.

Well, I should probably wrap up and say that this is an aspect of actor-network theory that to me seems very important, and I think that by shifting too quickly into a metaphysics of objects we might risk losing some of the progress made there. And also, if Latour says he's now going to do a metaphysics of the modes of existence, I can see that you get a more high-resolution philosophy that way, than by saying that we are going to look at all these events of which we understand so little. But this commitment is what I wanted to flag here. And then I have three points of discussion, which I'll try to summarize really quickly, and maybe in discussion they can be elaborated.

The first point is about ontology and epistemology; the relation or the slippage between them. Because again, one of the important points of actor-network theory was to problematize or perhaps in some cases suspend that distinction. It showed how from the description of entities we could get to the realization and the existence of entities. And I think that may also have important implications for the practice of philosophy itself. In order to do philosophy we don't need to say that we are thinking exclusively ontology or exclusively epistemology. Because that way of carving up the philosophical universe may actually also be an artifact of the age of human access that Graham I think rightly wants to move beyond.

The second point is about the social and political, in relation to the metaphysical. I think in Graham's book the political erupts at interesting moments and sometimes does things that maybe the author is also surprised by. But there are also points where politics becomes a model. So, for instance, the democracy of objects where politics is taken as a model and subsumed as a model in metaphysics. This idea of politics as reducible to a model or blueprint carries a risk, it seems to me: that of returning us to a legislative mode of theorizing politics that Latour's empiricism allows us to complicate. This also relates to a question that Alberto Toscano formulated. So what do we do with that?

The last point is about the definition of object. Because I think that when Graham says what his book does is to show that a theory of specific objects is where metaphysics has to go, this is a challenge that metaphysics must take on: how to theorize, how to engage specific objects. But if metaphysics takes on this challenge, what an object is must change, or become something different. And the fact that in the descriptions of actor-network theory we continuously encounter actant forces, affects, and at one point ANT even stated very clearly that an object is an effect. But if we engage in studying specific objects, we do not find this singularized thing that is well put-together, as an object. We do not find it at the foundation but we find it as an emergent effect. So a star system is an emerging effect; an architectural building is an emerging effect. How can metaphysics take in that kind of object and still be an object-orientated philosophy, which I think of course it must be.

Graham Harman

Which kinds of objects, again? Can you repeat the examples?

Noortje Marres

Star systems and architectural buildings. Let's take one of those fancy ones that are complicated and therefore imply all sorts of public relations and strange fashion statements.

Edgar Whitley
Do you want to respond now or wait for Lucas?

Graham Harman
Which is better?

Edgar Whitley
It is up to you whether you want to potentially deflect some of those questions…

Graham Harman
I might as well just deal with them now. Yes, actor-network theory might be a style of event-thinking. That is, they are punctuated events. It is not the sort of flow and becoming that you find as a primary feature of other philosophies. In Bruno's philosophy you could have long stretches of time when nothing happens. It's not really time. Time does not exist until an irreversible situation is created. So if someone wants to use the phrase "process philosophy" for what he's done, that's fine. I just don't want it to be confused with what the other people are doing. I don't want them all lumped in one basket, because I don't think they belong together.

Noortje Marres
Okay.

Graham Harman
I know we disagree about the meaning of this initial move of putting everything on the same footing. We even talked about this in Amsterdam during the [*Krisis*] interview.[43] For one thing, you think it's a starting point, I think it is already true that everything is

ontologically equal in real life. I just think that things are not equally *strong*. In Latour's philosophy, I think they are all equally *real*. But another possible point of disagreement is that you think the motive for that was the focus on change. I don't know what his real psychological motive was in doing it, but within the context of the theory the point of doing it seems to be that it allows us to focus more directly on individual actors. You can't focus on individual actors if you start with the primary difference between what kinds are real and what kinds aren't, that there are certain real physical entities and then certain figments that the human mind projects onto those. Bruno denounces this (no, I shouldn't say "denounce") *destroys* it so wonderfully in *We Have Never Been Modern*. Of course he never denounces anything, so I shouldn't use that word. So yes, I have a different reading of the importance of that move. I don't think it is so much about events.

As for the ontology/epistemology relation, that's pretty easy to handle because I don't believe in confusing them. I'm more traditional in that way. I do think there is a distinction, because I think epistemology has to do with our relations to things, and of course I think that the things themselves are outside the relations. That leaves two points. First, the social and political. Actually both of those points were well taken, especially because I usually don't like correlating ontological positions with political ones. I usually hate it when people do that, when people assume that relationality means progressive left-wing politics and substance means oppressive reactionary politics. [LAUGHTER] I usually hate that assumption. And so maybe I was too... a bit careless in the manuscript in equating ontological democracy with political democracy, although I think that connection is there in Bruno's work. Those two are often spoken of in the same register, especially in *Politics of Nature*. Democracy for Latour does seem to be the form of government best capable of dealing with these actors that don't know what each other are and are trying to take each other into account. And then after Alberto [Toscano] made his point about these non-progressive figures, Nietzsche and Tarde, who seemed to be great influences on *Irreductions*, I started rethinking this a bit. Could you have a totalitarian reading of actor-network theory? And could it be picked up for nefarious purposes? You know, "let the stronger actors prevail," or something like that. So I don't know. But I think I should have been a little more careful with that connection of ontology and politics, though.

The last point was about complicated objects. I'm not sure I understand the question. It's an interesting theme but I am not sure I understood what the problem was. How would it be so much harder to speak of complicated ones than of traditional ones, like horses and buckets [LAUGHTER] and the things that Aristotle talks about?

Bruno Latour
Hammers.

Graham Harman
Hammers.

Noortje Marres
Well, there are two different things at stake there. I think one has to do with complicated objects doing something with the metaphysical mode of defining what an object is. So, complicated objects continuously disturb definitions of what they are supposed to be like; they do not comply. So, what do you do with that? But the second point is that in the last part of your book there seems to be a situation... A situation comes about suggesting that Latour reduces objects to their effects, which are merely their attributes, which are therefore mere surface, and then you step in to save depth and give us substance again. And that's a sort of bifurcation, if you will. That seems to be a way in which object-oriented philosophy precisely cannot do one of the things that it should do, and aspires to, namely take these complicated objects which are

94

emergent and recognize them as the worthy objects of an object-oriented philosophy. See, you cut these complex emergent things in half and say there is some surface and there is some substance.

Graham Harman

But I'm also doing that with the simple things. I am doing that with chairs and horses also, so it is not like...

Noortje Marres

Yeah, those I don't mind. [LAUGHTER]

Graham Harman

I would agree that of course complicated objects are more problematic in terms of what their nature really is. I do want to stick with this bifurcation, but again I want to stick with it in objects of every level of size and complexity, that a thing has to be more than or different from its relations. And so that is a bifurcation I am willing to stick with. In fact I think it is the only one in my whole philosophy: the difference between objects and relations. And I think you can avoid that, but if you avoid that, then you avoid it by flattening everything out too much, so that everything is just on the level of its manifestation. And then that leads to these other philosophical paradoxes that I complained about before: you can't explain the change of the things and you can't explain the counterfactual situations of other possible observers and entities being in the vicinity. So I'm not really sure that the complicated objects pose a different sort of challenge to my theory than the simple ones do. I think you can accept or reject my theory on both levels for the same reasons. But I do agree that in *practical* terms complicated objects pose problems that Aristotle never saw. I mean, it is hard to imagine Aristotle's metaphysics covering star systems and the internet and how he would... It would be easy for him, he would just say those aren't substances, those are aggregates.

Noortje Marres

Yes.

Graham Harman

He can keep the substances simple by decree and not deal with them, not deal with the complicated ones.

Bruno Latour

Can I interrupt for a minute? But I think you actually mention in the manuscript something which is the heart of the argument in Fleck and in science studies, which is precisely that complicated objects are more metaphysically interesting because we cannot easily do for them what we do with hammers and with ordinary objects. And that's the point which has already been made by us that science and technology are actually easier to study because they are a complication and novelty. And the fact that they are not widespread, at least at the beginning, makes them better candidates to raise new questions, as I mentioned this morning about the case of the Veronese painting. Can I add one more thing? Because usually it's true, I mean this is a common thing in political philosophy, that reactionary thinkers are more interesting than the progressive ones [LAUGHTER] in that you learn more about politics from people like Machiavelli and [Carl] Schmitt than from Rousseau. And the exceptions are extremely rare, like [Walter] Lippmann (an example I owe to Noortje). But there is no connection, and I think that's an important point that Toscano makes, that there is actually no connection at all with the idea of the multiplicity of beings and any sort of democratic position because democracy, again, and I think that's something I learnt and I am working more and more with others at my political science school, it is a very, very, very, very different type of trajectory which I call political enunciation. It is completely specific, and which is actually not very much studied by people interested in democracy. I mean as a rule, apart from the great pragmatist tradition, it is a very epistemological definition of what it is to represent. So we should not confuse (and this is a great clarification made by Noortje) the idea of multiplicity of beings and the consequent abandonment of the human-nonhuman distinction with any position about how to organize the polity. This is an entirely different question and which relies on the specification of what is original in the political mode of existence, as different from law as it is from reference, and so on.

Graham Harman

But am I misremembering *Politics of Nature*? I seem to remember that the connection was implied: the justification of democracy in *Politics of Nature* did seem to be for ontological reasons.

Bruno Latour

But that might be the weakness of *Politics of Nature* that it gives this impression. Nietzsche and Tarde, as Toscano says, are not the greatest...

Graham Harman

...democrats. Yeah, yeah that's right.

Bruno Latour

I mean Tarde is different, Tarde is slightly different but...

Noortje Marres

And to add one more point, in relation to these complex objects, if you want to reintroduce all the questions of metaphysics that got buried in the Kantian age... Those questions cannot stay the same, you cannot say, "okay now the Ice Age is over and I dig up my roots and seeds and I'll grow the same plants again." And one reason or the principal reason this is so is precisely made clear by actor-network theory right from the start, namely that the industrial world is one where the answer to the question of what exists is fundamentally variable. Now it's a dynamic world where suddenly a new element can be added to the periodic table. So it's about... how can metaphysics turn that into something productive for metaphysics rather than something challenging to it against which it must be defended. You see?

Graham Harman

The answer is: by not placing the essences on a level that is easy to debunk. I feel the same way about Bruno's invocation of Darwin. That obviously was very important for him and for a number of thinkers of the same stripe. And I would agree that the metaphysical questions cannot come back in the same form as before Kant. They have to be modified to fit the new situation and it would take hard work. But they don't need to be swept away into this agnostic night [LAUGHTER] where they have been left for 220 years. And Bruno said he agreed about this anyway, that the metaphysical questions should be brought back.

Bruno Latour

We need that.

Graham Harman

But you think they have to be solved politically? This was a ...

Bruno Latour

I know, I won't argue with you.

Graham Harman

Okay, okay.

Lucas Introna

That may be a good point for me. When I was thinking about posing some problems that would be common to you and Bruno I was imagining that if we accept the idea that Bruno has an empirical metaphysics and you have a Heideggerian metaphysics, then a question that came up in my mind is: can we make this metaphysics act in the practice of doing research? In more pragmatic terms, does it make a difference to the sorts of things I might do when I do my experiments? And if it doesn't, then maybe the metaphysical question is not an important question in that respect and can be set aside. So we don't have to start our theses by writing our chapter on metaphysics before we do the description. If it does make a difference, then in a way I would be interested to know what that difference would be.

The other point is that if you read many of the questions that were sent in [ahead of time by symposium participants], I think what is very clear is that there is the point Bruno made earlier that one of the flaws in *Irreductions* was the fact that it had difficulty explaining trajectory, or rather accounting for trajectory. And in his address to the British Sociological Association, he says "All the same, it's a great weakness for a theory to claim that every mode of connection is specific, while at the same time not being able to say in what way each mode differs from the others,"[44] also touches on this question of trajectory and duration, of durability. That although every event is specific, there is some continuity between events. Because if that were not the case, everything would be unprecedented, everything would have to be done from scratch. It would be like natural scientists repeating the same experiments again and again because they've learnt nothing from any previous experiments. Clearly they have. So something carries over from experiment to experiment. So even though we have serial description, the serial description is not from scratch every time, since description takes something from previous descriptions, if you take description as a new experimental metaphor that has been used.

So it seems to me that one of the important consequences of that is that, as Bruno acknowledged, you end up with the problem of giving an account of some metaphysics in which you have to give an account of different modes of existence. And in a sense, is the account of different modes of existence an acknowledgement that actor-network theory means metaphysics?

Bruno Latour

Yes... [LAUGHTER] I begin to feel a slight horror toward this notion of the *punctual* because I wonder if it is true even of the most traditional actor-network theory. Noortje reminded us of the notion of event and you mentioned it. It's always the beginning of a trajectory; it's a vector. It seems to me that I have always been interested in vectors. So, no matter how small the point we study, it actually has a vector quality. Now, in the old days of... What did you say of Kant? An Ice...

Noortje Marres

Ice Age.

Bruno Latour

Ice Age, thank you ..., before global warming... [LAUGHTER]— the Ice Age, we could not really capture this vector notion because we were bifurcated by this "might and right" division, materialism, and so on. But now it's quite possible to do the vector. So the second point you made, I actually think it's quite interesting to see that when you say "carried over from one moment to the next," the carrier is what I want to study. So the type of carrier is very different if it is a small van or a bicycle or one of these guys who are bringing pizza to you, and so on. And that's what in the old days I defined as the heart, the paradigm of information systems: namely, how many ways there are to carry over from one time to the next. But this was invisible if you suppose... this is a point of Tarde against Durkheim again, if you suppose that a "society" exists, the carrier disappears. So the enormous weight to maintain the existence, to the subsistence, is immediately replaced by a substance which hides behind it. And of course, as Graham said too, that's the difficulty I have with sticking to bifurcation.

Now the first point you made: what difference does it make in terms of empirical research? It makes the whole difference if actors or events are not allowed to have their own metaphysics. My problem with the social sciences is that the repertoire that they accept in the world, of action, of theory of space, of a theory of time, of the definition of what an individual is, of the whole basic furniture of the world, is set in advance. If you read even critical theorists, the list of what is supposed to exist is already fixed. So for example I am very interested in religion. I can say that the anthropology of religion is no use to me because it begins by saying, "of course all of these gods and divinities are not there, they cannot be part of the entities that exist." What's the use of doing any study in anthropology of religion if you fix at the beginning and say: "well, of course we know that all these fetishes are just representations in the minds of people." By the way, in your book you never refer to the study of fetishes, factishes.[45]

Graham Harman

In this book I didn't.

Bruno Latour

It is an issue where construction and reality are actually intertwined. So this is why, for me, maybe to get a varied nuance between what ... I mean he is a professional metaphysician, I'm not ... Again, I am running to the wolves by following philosophers this way... [MAKES HOWLING SOUND] [LAUGHTER]. So they go, ha-ha-ha, howl, this guy is lucky... But I think it is quite important that I then become a real metaphysician in the very simple sense of saying: if you don't read the philosophers, and don't read the wrong ones, read the right ones. If you don't read the right ones, whenever you have someone who comes to you and says, to use my favorite example: "I come here because they fabricate better Gods," you will be stuck. You will have no resources to understand the extraordinary invention, the inventiveness of this lady who comes to a convent to fabricate gods, because we are supposed to separate fabrication and belief. It is the same with the Veronese story I told this morning.

So of course professional metaphysicians might object to that because it is a bit of a toolbox. And they might say, well, metaphysics is more serious than just allowing you to do fieldwork. And I think they are right because once you have done the fieldwork, there might be feedback from the fieldwork to metaphysics. And my study of factishes, which is a complete failure as an invented term... I have run another round of social constructivism all the way again, but it was exactly that. Okay, now that we have understood that it's possible for actors themselves to articulate constructivism as a cause of reality, what does it change for the study of religion? And of course theologians became even more incensed than philosophers of science about what I said about religion. But for me this travel back and forth is what I would call metaphysical help for the fieldwork. But of course, none of that would produce serious, professionally publishable metaphysics in a journal, in *Mind* or in *Revue de métaphysique et de morale*.

Graham Harman

They would never accept my stuff either. [LAUGHTER]

Edgar Whitley

Do you want to respond Graham?

Graham Harman

Yes, two points. First of all, I'm still not sure how you get to vectors if you say a thing happens in one time and one place only, unless you are just saying: "that's just *Irreductions*, it wasn't good enough."

Bruno Latour

Because things are famished. They're just, they're just... Have you ever seen a punctual event? [LAUGHTER] Which is not sent, which is not carried, which is not arced out?

Graham Harman
I haven't seen it, but now you are just talking about something else. I was talking about a trajectory across time, which is a different thing.

Bruno Latour
No. Don't things have descendants and ascendants? I am surprised by this reading of punctuality, because I don't think that's the spirit of networks. The whole notion of the network is something that passes; not because it is in time but because it has descendants and ascendants.

Graham Harman
That's fine, but it's a different question from time. And if you say that a thing happens in one time and one place only, you are saying that it is cut off punctually in an instant.

Bruno Latour
But I am not saying it happened once. I said it happens once: it's irreducible, which is not exactly the same notion.

Graham Harman
You do say that it happens only once.

Bruno Latour
Well, maybe I said so. [LAUGHTER]

Edgar Whitley
But didn't necessarily mean it. [LAUGHTER]

Alberto Toscano

He said it once, in one place only... [LAUGHTER]

Graham Harman

As far as what difference it would make... I was asked this question also by Maha [Shaikh] after the November lecture:[46] what implications would this have for method? And I didn't really have a good answer then. I have been thinking about it a bit ever since. It's for people who do the fieldwork to see if they read this book and are inspired to try a new method. I don't know what that would be. But one thing I sometimes suspect is that the method of hidden substances would be better for dealing with counterfactual situations. I don't want to just throw that out there, in case there are people in ANT already doing it and I am insulting their work by not knowing about it. But it just seems to me that thinking of things as events or relations is better when they have already happened; it's more instructive when they have already happened and you look at what the factors were in those events. But let's imagine, how would today's colloquium have been different if we had added the following people to the audience: [Slavoj] Žižek, my brother, and some third person? What other things might have happened today that didn't happen? What sorts of questions might have been asked that were not? I think you can't really do that if you look at today just as an event that was made up of the actors who made it possible. It is a little more than that, too. There is also something in today's event that was created by all those actors that nonetheless exceeds those actors: so that other actors could have come and fed on it and added to it. And I don't think that is completely nonsensical. Historians sometimes try this kind of...

Bruno Latour

But, can I say it, even though because... there is this extraordinary passage in Deleuze's *Différence et Répétition*[47] which always struck me very deeply. Which is lightning [MAKES SOUND], when the lightning strikes, the lightning and the night are visible. So you dismiss... I am surprised because Deleuze makes a great deal of the difference between potentiality and virtuality, and of the opposition between the two couples potential and real, and virtual and actual. And you say that this is hair-splitting or something. I mean you say it is not...

Graham Harman

No, not hair-splitting, it just doesn't solve the problem I have in mind.

Bruno Latour

But why? Because then it seems to me that... isn't this a way out of the actualist argument that potential is really the enemy... and that's why I said one thing arrives once only, but was against (I've read my Deleuze quite carefully and have the same admiration for Péguy) is that the potential/real opposition means that the real is nothing, because everything is already potential and the real is just a small deformation. And we know that very well in information systems, in management, in epistemology and politics and so on. "Give me the potential, the real will follow." But if you take the other couple, which is virtual and actual (actual is a bit of a misnomer because of the actualism argument) it is a very, very, very different type of connection. If the striking lightning is there (and it's a completely positivist point) the virtuality accompanies it. This is the argument of Deleuze when he said that until the flowers are there, the sun is not the cause of the flowers. It's only once the flowers have appeared that the causality of the sun becomes extremely important. So the cause of the flowers goes back, so to speak, inside the causality of the sun. So the difficulty is that if you take an irreductionist point, I agree it is very difficult to articulate that, and there is an actualism built into it. And that's what I consider to be the main mistake, the limitation of *Irreductions*. But it is not the same thing as to say that things are not vectors, because being a vector is what it is, to be is to be, trying to survive or trying... This is a *conatus*.

So as for punctuality, I think it's unfair to talk about punctuality, because what would a punctual event be? I can't really understand it. It would be something which had no ascendants, no descendants, no wish to survive, no anything. It would be what?

Graham Harman

You can't create time by borrowing from *conatus*. *Conatus* could in principle be confined within a moment. It might be hard to visualize, but there is nothing in *conatus* that says there has to be a flow of time, the kind that Bergson talks about.

Bruno Latour

Not a flow but a descendant.

Graham Harman

No, there just has to be an outward-directedness, and that could happen punctually. *Conatus* doesn't imply that there is any unfolding of time. For you, time is created by actors. That is not the case with Bergson. For him, time is not created by actors.

Bruno Latour

But ... rabbits have kids.

Graham Harman

Yeah, but ... [LAUGHTER]

Bruno Latour

The vector quality is really what actor-network tried to grasp in some sort of sense. Badly, I agree, with the notion of irreduction, but...

Noortje Marres

But wasn't it also the point that in order for an object to happen or to come about, you have the building of trajectories... I mean, I think now of John Law who wrote this paper on long distance control in the Portuguese sea trade.[48] It is all about how these sea routes came about, how the ships came about, how they figured out ways to build ships that could endure over these distances, navigation, all these things that are actually part of the story of the spice trade. So if you want to get to spices, you have to take that whole trajectory, that whole circulatory arrangement into account. By talking about how an object happens in only one time and place and by assuming that an actor is concrete, this whole infrastructural aspect is lost from view. So you see that suddenly all sorts of things become mysterious to the philosopher, if you don't consider this trajectory-building aspect that is essential to the circulation of an object, and cannot really be distinguished from it in any simple way.

Graham Harman

But trajectories have to be...

Noortje Marres

...articulations of objects.

Graham Harman

Trajectories have to be created by outside actors, right? It is an outside actor who determines that a thing is the same thing as it was...

Bruno Latour

No, things are expectant. I mean you said I was a secular occasion-alist, right?

Graham Harman

Secular occasionalist, yes.

Bruno Latour
So, Allah is in every single expectant occasion, right?

Graham Harman
For?

Bruno Latour
Secular, if I am secular ... Every single entity is expectant of a next step.

Graham Harman
Not expectant, but it becomes a possible mediator of any other two entities.

Bruno Latour
No, but for itself, we are talking about the thing itself. It is expectant, is it not?

Graham Harman
I don't think it is expectant. I don't know where this expectation is coming in, this *conatus*. I don't think it solves the time problem. I think it is a totally separate issue. But I want to say something about the virtual. The reason I'm never impressed by philosophies of the virtual, whether it is Deleuze or DeLanda or the few times I have heard you use it in conversation, is that it's an attempt to shift the action away from the individual objects and put it somewhere else. Then all of a sudden these individual objects are already completely deployed, they are sterile, they are on the surface, so let's move discussion somewhere else. Why? Why do we have to think that the individual objects lack this power? Why does everybody agree that the individual object has nothing held in reserve? I agree that it's not potential because I think to call something potential means it has the potential to relate to other things, which I want to stay away from. It has to be something in its

own right. But why call it virtual? Why not just grant each thing that non-related depth?

Bruno Latour

But isn't that what occasionalism is all about? If it is not a causality, it is an occasion, which means there is an enormous reserve for other occasions. When chlorophyll is invented, the sun never imagined that chlorophyll was invented. The sun is not the cause of chlorophyll. Now that chlorophyll is here, the sun is the cause of chlorophyll. But there are lots of other things that flowers can do.

Graham Harman

This is retroactive causality, not occasional causality. I think there is a difference. Because occasionalism considers a real situation where something is linking to other things. This retroactivity, I think, is somewhat different. I'm not sure I can articulate it well.

Bruno Latour

So am I an occasionalist or not?

Graham Harman

Yeah. [LAUGHTER] Because things happen in one time and one place only, even if you regret having said that.

Bruno Latour

No, I like it.

Graham Harman

Oh! [LAUGHTER]

Bruno Latour

I like it, but it is a small vector, though it is still a vector. It can be very small, but it still has an arrow at the end.

Graham Harman

But that doesn't mean it points outside that moment of time; it just means that it points outside of itself.

Bruno Latour

One does look very carefully to how it might subsist, knowing that there is no substance anymore. See, that's the big problem of philosophy. Substance was a very nice way of solving all our questions, right? And then you have the primary, the secondary qualities floating around and substance was doing the job of subsistence. Okay. We took substance away. Now why we did that might be disputable and I think in this building there will be lots of people who will dispute it. [LAUGHTER] Because substance would be...

Okay, we now have to pay our way in order to subsist. And if you want to do that, it means that you have to be very, very worried constantly about how you are going to pay your way. If a horse (and this is a Darwinian argument)... if the horse is not there to subsist, to make the horse subsist, every horse has to do its own maintenance, so to speak. Now that's true also for this and that and here and everywhere. Now what I add to that is that there might be many, many... fortunately not too many different ways of subsisting. But the vector quality, the expectant, expected, expectancy of beings seems to me a common theme which would be very difficult to take out of the whole of the philosophical tradition. Because then the notion of an atomic event which has no successor, no predecessor, is that not something we learn from atomism? I mean, from the Epicureans? Is it not something that already has the skeptics, skepticism in view? Is this true?

Graham Harman

That atomism already paves the way for skepticism?

Bruno Latour

Yeah. Isn't there already a long history of philosophy behind you when you get the idea that you have atoms?

Graham Harman

Oh sure, they were fairly late in the pre-Socratic tradition, the atomists. First you have air, water, fire-air-earth-water mixed by love and hate, and atomism is almost the last phase that is contemporary with Socrates himself. But it's the one that's triumphed. It is the one out of all the pre-Socratic philosophies that has triumphed, and it is taken as common sense now. But it took a long time to make atoms seem like common sense.

Lucas Introna

Yeah, but in terms of Heideggerian philosophy, Heidegger talks about *Dasein* as being projected, as always already projected, always already expecting. That we anticipate the future, we don't simply walk out the door and be surprised by what's on the other side of the door. In walking to the door we already anticipate what's on the other side of the door. What you are suggesting is, and I think you would agree, is the idea that all actors are expectant, all actors are projected. But we anthropomorphize it by saying 'expectant.' Because how is the table expectant? But of course it is expectant, inasmuch as it has a certain sense in which it is its being, its mode of existence.

Graham Harman

And here I want to interject and say that Heidegger is an absolute occasionalist and has no theory of time despite "time" being included in the title *Being and Time* [LAUGHTER]. I can say pretty easily why. There is projection in Heidegger, but it doesn't give him time. He is the best proof of what I'm talking about. Compare Heidegger and Bergson on time. For Heidegger, if you are talking about a succession of instants, that's the vulgar theory of temporality, right. When you are talking about death, if you talk about an actual date on the calendar when you are going to die, that's the vulgar concept of death. The real concept of death means the death that influences you right now in this very moment. It influences your comportment toward the world right now. And the future and past for Heidegger are the ones in the "right now." It is not anything having to do with a stream or flow of time or even a vector. Well, maybe he would call it a vector. But it isn't anything that takes him out of the instant, that's why he talks about the *Augenblick*, the moment, which is so important in his philosophy. Heidegger really is just a philosopher of a succession of instants. There is no flow between them, and this is why the conflation of Heidegger with Bergson drives me up the wall. The two are so different. Heidegger even *says* that Bergson is guilty of the vulgar concept of time in a whole chapter in *Being and Time*, and people just ignore that and say yeah, Heidegger and Bergson agree that you can't break time down into instants. That's nonsense, because that's *all* that Heidegger does. He just breaks time down into a series of statuesque poses and he never connects them, which is fine, you pay a price...

Bruno Latour
So what sort of occasionalist is he, in your view? Is he a secular occasionalist?

Graham Harman
Absolutely not. Yes, you are all alone. [LAUGHTER]

Bruno Latour
No, I was worried... [LAUGHTER]

Graham Harman
They'll give you a gold medallion. [LAUGHTER] You're an occasionalist. [LAUGHTER]

Bruno Latour

I need a certificate. [LAUGHTER]

Edgar Whitley

A couple of questions. One, two and three.

Alberto Toscano

I just wanted to... because I think it's obviously a quite crucial issue, to press you on this distinction between objects and relations. Now, it seems at least from the account that you give of Latour's notion of the black box that at least within the metaphysics here someone could easily see a way in which that distinction might exist but it might just be a relative distinction...

Graham Harman

Yeah...

Alberto Toscano

... i.e. an object is a relation that has yet to be opened up for investigations, trials of strength and what have you. And you can think of lots of different ways of thinking the distinction between objects and relations that are relative distinctions, whereby some forms of scientific activity would just involve treating relations as objects, or objects as relations, and so on and so forth. Now obviously, because of the metaphysical desiderata that you have, you want to say that this is a real distinction and not a relative one.

Graham Harman

Yeah...

Alberto Toscano

But I was wondering how that fits in with one of the things that I think is most interesting about your approach, and your reading of Latour as well, which is the denial of any obvious notion of scale.

So there is not any obvious sense in which... You seem at times to say that okay, I think at times to say that actors are within other actors, so that already confuses me and stuff. Well, if they are within other actors, then how are objects separate from relations, that seemed to be already a peculiar issue.

And there also doesn't seem to be any account as to why... if every relation itself is an object, then the whole account of occasionalism seems to disappear because... or is in fact so... enters into such an infinite regress because even the relations and objects have themselves to be related... So it seems to me that the problems generated by wanting to maintain that as a real, as opposed to a relative distinction.... I can see for the purposes of research how the distinction between an actor and a network sort of makes immediate and intuitive sense. But when you give examples, I don't see why when you give lists of things that are objects, why you couldn't... continue those lists by adding things that we might intuitively think are relations. And so I don't see anything that would keep the relation from turning into an object under certain circumstances. And that seems to be an important issue for the relationship between the metaphysics and the methodologies.

Graham Harman
The first step of my answer would be to say that yes, any object can be thought of in terms of relation because any object is a black box that has countless interior components. But to say that it's dependent on those is a different sort of thing from saying it's dependent on its outer relations. Once a thing is created, it's there. And it doesn't really matter how it was created, it's a unit. It was somehow able to unify all those parts and become one thing. You can argue about what the definition of one thing is. But that is different from saying that it's dependent on all the effects it has on other things. In other words, there's a kind of asymmetry between the relations that make up the thing and the relations in which it later engages. The thing itself is almost like a...

Alberto Toscano

Like genetic relations and…

Graham Harman

Yeah, but genetic implies over time, so I would say it is more a… I think the thing has to be free from its outer relations but it can't be free of its inner relations. I don't want to call them internal or external because it is not the same thing. I speak of "domestic relations," all the parts that make up the thing I call its domestic relations, rather than its internal relations, which has a different meaning. Because otherwise what you would have is just an infinite fusion in which all the things in the universe fuse together into a big chain. There wouldn't be any point where substance or individuals existed, because you'd just have all these relations adding up in a flash to the universe as a whole. The reason there are individual objects is because an individual object is kind of a plug: it is a unifying thing that requires all of its parts to exist, but then it doesn't necessarily have to engage in any of these other relations. It maintains a certain identity, a certain privacy, no matter what other outer relations it engages in. So that's the first part of my answer.

Oh, the next one was about objects and relations. I do think that any real relation automatically becomes an object. Once two terms somehow manage to relate it does become an object. And the reason I think this is because if you try to make up a list of what the features of an object are, and of a relation, they actually share the same features…

Alberto Toscano

So there are no such things as freely floating relations?

Graham Harman

That's right. Once they're made, they are an object because they have all the features they need of an object, they have a unified character, they are inexhaustible by any description…

Alberto Toscano
But then they are only objects, in which case I don't see why you would have occasionalism in the first place.

Graham Harman
Because not all…

Alberto Toscano
…they are not relating anything…

Graham Harman
…because you have a bunch of objects that are not related yet, and in order to get them together you need to somehow find a mechanism by which they fuse into a new object. That's the only role outer relations really play. Yeah, it's just objects, and nothing but objects, and all the objects are contained inside other objects.

Bruno Latour
But I want to disagree with the first part of your answer again, because to pursue this experiment started by Peter on what difference it makes to metaphysics, your answer for me makes sense but then it contradicts what I am interested in. For example, the biologists Sonigo and Kupiec wrote a book, which is called *Ni Dieu ni gène*,[49] which criticizes what they call the Aristotelian version of information as a metaphor for biological systems. And they say the genetics metaphor of information and signal is actually a transportation into biology, into secular biology of Aristotle's God, used for the notion of information. Now they open inside biology itself the question which should not be settled, which is: what is an organism? So they move from the forest, the body metaphor for a forest metaphor. This question is a huge area of dispute inside biology, not only because we are made of many cells and the cells

themselves are made of many cells, but because the very notion of information as transportation of signals might be disputable for a real hardcore Darwinian like Sonigo is. So, here are two different answers... if I take just the answer that Graham gave you and my answer, this would be my way to pursue a different emphasis. I would again call metaphysics the question that follows this very interesting book by Sonigo, opening the very question of what is a whole, and the relation between the whole and part in organisms. We should not close this question too quickly. And the people who are in information systems... I mean not the information systems in this sense but the information paradigm in genetics, have closed much too quickly the question in biology of what an organism is. As Sonigo shows very nicely, biologists are Darwinians for the whole organism, but inside the organism they are the most completely traditional Aristotelians, who suppose that people send signals, and then cells send the... They make fun of this argument that cells actually wait for a signal before committing suicide because there is a master plan somewhere. Biologists basically have imported the thing which we would never dare to teach to our management students here because it would be a completely outdated version of what an organism is in organization, and yet the notion still persists inside biology. So my definition of metaphysics is this: what is the metaphysics which can open this question enough, so that we can follow the dispute in this part in biology. Does that clarify our discussion about this?

Graham Harman
Yeah.

Bruno Latour
Because that's the heart of two different aspects of metaphysics. We need these guys because it is precisely they who provide us with the tool which allows us to keep open, inside the most basic hard science question, the settlement of that very dispute that you very

nicely mentioned. And if you take Gaia and then again the whole question of "are we an organism or inside a big organism?" is the question that Lovelock opened. So, those are the very practical consequences for me of what I would call metaphysics.

Chrisanthi Avgerou
Listening to all this I'm trying very hard to understand the Latourian notion of serial description...

Bruno Latour
It's that gentleman's notion... [POINTING AT MICHAEL WITMORE] [LAUGHTER]

Chrisanthi Avgerou
...which nevertheless you accepted. And also, you have written yourself that descriptions are actually the legitimate thing to do. 'Description' is a deceptively simple, probably innocent word that appears devoid not only of metaphysics, but also of other assumptions and choices. And yet from the way you describe your efforts here to understand the vector that you are interested in and reflect on the way we all study whatever vectors we study, it seems to me that it's difficult to go very far with descriptions. Indeed, what you have described here is your view about the damage done by social sciences so far, which you want to overcome, and this involves choices about the manner of your descriptions: for example, not to bother with the wastebasket but to concentrate on other things, and then to go back to making metaphysical kind of claims. How can all of this be packaged in a description of what we do, which of course mystifies the whole effort of doing research? I think it is important to try to unpack and to reveal the theoretical and metaphysical questions. How much unpacking this requires still remains very opaque to me because I am not a philosopher. But definitely, there is much more there than description, and I think it has to be articulated.

Bruno Latour

You are right. You are perfectly right that it is slightly disingenuous to call description the most difficult task of metaphysics... But I would stick to the word, because description is the most difficult thing to do, and precisely because it requires all of those skills, precisely because it requires so much metaphysics just to find the right description. If I take this example again, can you imagine that you go to all of the laboratories not only in this country but in other countries, and explain that whenever there is a notion of the signal in biology, it's a misdescription, and it is Aristotle's God which is actually brought in here and that this paper should be rejected from *The Lancet*, from *Nature*, [LAUGHTER] from *Cell Biology* and so on? And yet this is what is at stake. It's very difficult to describe a biological system, let alone describing an organization and information systems. So I still stick to the idea that even though I agree that my vocabulary is slightly disingenuous, and was troubling to students of information systems, if memory serves, it is important not to call it theory plus description. The whole theory should be the servant, the ancillary of a description of some sort. Because if not, then we will again be back in the traditional social sciences. So I agree that it's disingenuous, and that not everything can be putative. But it's description in the actor-network sense of the word, and that includes the whole of metaphysics.

Chrisanthi Avgerou

Doesn't that at least require revealing your starting point?

Bruno Latour

Oh, I do. This is why the Pasteur book has two parts; this is why *Aramis* is made of two parts. I've never hidden that. What I've hidden is this other... what did you call that, the second Latour?

Graham Harman

The later Latour... [LAUGHTER]

Bruno Latour

I agree. Here I have been hiding myself in a very unfair way. But I've always said that to do good description you need to do good metaphysics. That's why this guy here [POINTS AT GRAHAM HARMAN] is taking seriously the metaphysics but not the description. [LAUGHTER]

Maha Shaikh

I'm not a philosopher, I don't know anything about philosophy but you've been talking about potentiality and then I think Lucas mentioned expectancy as well. I don't understand these terms really, to be honest. What does potentiality mean? Do you mean that it has to interact? Could I go as far as to suggest that potentiality could mean "agency" and "expectancy" on some level of intentionality or... What does that mean, and what's the relationship?

Graham Harman

Well, as you might notice, Bruno rejects potentiality but does not reject expectancy. Expectancy for him would be a vector, something that is pointing outwards. Whereas he always rejects potentiality because this allows a thing to borrow its achievements in advance without paying for them. Aristotle introduces potentiality to explain the fact that things change, things move, while still remaining the same thing. An acorn becomes an oak tree.

There were rival philosophers, the Megarians, who said: "no, a thing only is what it is right now." And so if someone is not building a house right now, he is not a house builder, even if he has expertise but is currently sleeping. He is not a house builder because he is not doing it right now. Aristotle says this is absurd, because this implies that an educated but sleeping house builder is the same as a totally ignorant house builder. But there has to be some way to account for the difference between these, and so for Aristotle potentiality is very important. I tend to reject it along with

Bruno, however, because I think it is an attempt to avoid the question of where that potentiality lies *in the actual*. What is it in the actual that enables it to change, and in Bruno's case he wants… you have to show the step-by-step translations that allow the person to build the house. You can't say it had a magic potential in advance, because for Bruno every step of the translation is very important. Saying that "the oak tree was potentially in the acorn" means that you allow yourself to skip the difficult question of what all the phases were. I think you said in a few beautiful images in *Irreductions* that it's as stupid as saying that the dessert is already implicitly contained in the recipe… You even said something more controversial, that [people are wrong to think that] all the proofs of Euclid are implicitly contained in the axioms, which is what some people do think. But for Bruno you have to spell out each step of the translation, do the work at each step to show it. And I think this is what Netz's book is all about, right?

Bruno Latour
On that I agree entirely with you.

Graham Harman
Okay, so we both reject potentiality.

Bruno Latour
But intentionality?

Graham Harman
I think you were accepting it as a kind of *conatus*…

Bruno Latour
This is intentional, yeah… [LIFTS PLASTIC CUP]

Graham Harman
Yeah, it is a kind of *conatus*. And I was saying you can't…

Bruno Latour

If that analogy is extended to everything, it's fine with me.

Maha Shaikh

How though?

Bruno Latour

Well, it has some sort of low expectancy [HOLDS UP PLASTIC CUP] [LAUGHTER] but because it was not granted much agency either. It is actually a lot of work to make it low expectancy. Cheap, what we call cheap.

Maha Shaikh

So it gained it from some other actor, through a relationship?

Bruno Latour

Yes, but it is now granted to this. Actually ecology is interesting because now this low and cheap expectancy, I mean [TAPS PLASTIC CUP] this cheap product can be redesigned in very interesting ways now, so that it has another intentionality, so to speak: the cheapness of it, the recyclability… All these words which are interesting now: *durable, sustainable*. So immediately you see another metaphysical object coming on, if they have to be sustainable, if they have to be politically correct, if they have to be ecologically correct. Again, the shift between agencies, and it is not just us. I mean it's not we humans making projections onto this thing. We actually produce very, very different objects now. And we are going to redesign all of our production in that way. So intentionality is a good word if it's extended to everything.

Graham Harman

Yes, we agree on that too.

Bruno Latour

Including the billiard ball that misunderstands the other billiard ball and skims only the surface of it.

Graham Harman

Yes, yes.

Bruno Latour

I love this part of the book.

Graham Harman

[LAUGHS] Yeah.

Bruno Latour

A ball just bumps into the other and just sees "obstacle." That's a great but difficult argument.

Lucas Introna

This is one way to talk about the cup having intentionality. In science and technology studies we use the term *affordance*. It affords certain things. I mean, it can't fly. There are many things it can't do. But it affords certain things. It was designed to afford certain things, and in that sense it has intentionality.

Maha Shaikh

I'm just thinking, do we not give it cognitive abilities if we say intentionality?

Lucas Introna

That's just a particular…

Bruno Latour

I thought it was a good term because what worries this lady is that it's our intention to build it, but once it's built it's…

Lucas Introna

A force...

Bruno Latour

...if not, it will not be built.

Graham Harman

But the short answer is yes. There is a big controversy over this, over whether you can have intentionality without implying panpsychism. This conflict is very much alive. Some people say yes, some people say no.

Edgar Whitley

Right, we have got time for one, maybe two quick questions that will have short answers if that is possible [LAUGHTER].

Isabelle Doucet

I'd like to link the question back to the datascapes that came in yesterday in Bruno Latour's lecture.[50] I am wondering if the notion of plasma that was mentioned earlier today would become more understandable if you thought of a dimensional, spatial way of writing, or even, a spatial way of representing the data or the descriptions that we get as a way of assembling things. If you look at examples of cartography, of mapping, the spatiality of this medium makes the plasma perfectly understandable all of a sudden; more than the work of assemblage and re-assemblage through mere textual descriptions. For example in cartography, the whole question today is that technically almost everything is possible. But it is the same as Graham's question. What is included in the map? Where is the plasma in the cartography? That's a very important question for anyone involved in datascapes and mapping. And I was wondering if this is something that could be a more spatial way of organizing? That this could also be linked back to a different type of writing...

Graham Harman

Where is the plasma in cartography? It sounds interesting. I'm not sure I have it yet, though.

Isabelle Doucet

For me there is... Even if you map all sorts of assemblages of the different elements of the spectrum of data, there is always what they call in cartography the "outfall," which is the unknown, which is kind of there but not yet included in the network because it is not yet formatted, not yet accounted for, perhaps simply not considered important. And then there are certain mapmakers who for example develop ways to represent this type of data, even if it is unknown, that is not yet known through the accepted forms of representation.

Bruno Latour

But your problem is that Google Earth came in.

Isabelle Doucet

Right.

Bruno Latour

And then, just at the time when we were finally using cartography as a good metaphor of the emptiness...

Isabelle Doucet

Yeah.

Bruno Latour

...Google Earth came in and then we lost it entirely because now the zoom is so easy that people are being prejudiced to think that the map is the territory again. I love Google Earth, even though the hotel I went to is misplaced on Google Earth. [LAUGHTER] Euro Hotel is misplaced on Google Earth. It's quite interesting, and I went to the wrong place but… And of course I knew that the map is not the territory. But the navigation of Google Earth is actually counter to what you say because there it seemed to me that the zoom is what the world is about. So we now have the social sciences equivalent in geography of the notion *to zoom*, which is very unfortunate, just at the precise time when the art and the production of maps were freeing us from the idea that the map was the territory. And that's slightly worrying.

Lucas Introna
If there aren't any other questions then I'd…

Edgar Whitley
Nobody's… I mean I think there are millions of questions and no questions, so… take advantage of being at the front.

Lucas Introna
I was very interested in the problem of trajectory. And one of the interesting things for me in *Reassembling the Social* was early on, when you make a distinction between transportation and transformation, and you make it very clear that to mediate is to transform. But later on when you get to the later chapters, you bring in transportation again when you talk about form. So one of the things I was wondering is whether it would not be more appropriate to say that translations always transport and transform at the same time. That there is always a residual in the translation. And it is exactly this residual in the translation that is transported rather than transformed that provides the basis for continuity. Going back to the experimental metaphor, when a social science experiment is set up, the next experiment obviously doesn't replicate that experiment but takes some residual which might be the data, might be some of the experimental set up or something, into the next experiment but

transforms the experiment, translating it into some new experiment. So, would it not be a way to account for the continuity, the trajectory, by admitting from the start that all translations transform and transport at the same time?

Bruno Latour

Well, but the problem is that there are many ways to be continuous and discontinuous. And the reference chains that I have been calling "immutable mobiles" for many years are one very, very specific way of being transported and transformed. And as I showed yesterday, the legal connectedness has absolutely no... I mean it is completely different because it is discontinuous, but it doesn't have the same continuity either. And it would again be very, very different from the Darwinian genealogy of rabbits and its genealogy of the acorn and the shell. So it is true generally, but the enemy here is clearly "information double-click," where there would be no transformation and transportation. But then the problem is to qualify, to specify the type of discontinuity and continuity. And it is very difficult to do that inside information theory now, because it is a very new, very strange beast. And I am not talking about religion and politics, which are even more bizarre, and organization is even more bizarre than all of these put together. I don't actually use translation very much either, because that's done easily. But the question of specifying the type of discontinuity and continuity is very much what I am trying to do now. And it is very difficult. I find it very, very difficult.

Of course in the history of philosophy as a whole, the whole shibboleth, the whole benchmark was the idea of demonstration. That's why I think the book by Reviel Netz is absolutely crucial for the history of philosophy because it is the first time we have a first-hand account, twenty-four centuries later, of a nonformal description of formalism. And he shows very nicely that Plato actually didn't know that much mathematics, but uses this idea of transportation without deformation as the ideal way of speaking of

127

all the big questions of philosophy. And Netz shows that in exquisite detail, the geometers, the two and a half geometers born every year for two centuries were extraordinarily careful to make absolutely no meta-geometric, meta-mathematical comments. Plato arrives, okay, and makes a big Hollywood blockbuster! [LAUGHTER] And now we have another way, now we are getting into the agora and we have another way of speaking which is the transporter without deformation. So it is true that this notion of information without transportation is... I think I was right, at a very young age, to say that this is an immutable mobile and that's a crucial thing, and I should spend thirty years trying to understand it. [LAUGHTER] But I could not understand the part which is on geometry, Greek geometry, and Reviel Netz did this fabulous book about that. My review of the book is on my website[51] for those who are interested.

Lucas Introna

Well, one can see the attractiveness of transportation without trans- formation.

Bruno Latour

Yes, it is substance!

Lucas Introna

Yes.

Bruno Latour

It solved the question of duration! It solved the question of political order! It solved the question of law! The Greek world would be silly not to use it. And yet what Reviel Netz shows is that in fact the allusions to geometry in the whole Greek corpus are extremely small. Medicine everywhere, law everywhere, politics everywhere, but geometry and mathematics are only in the Aristotelian and Platonist tradition. It is very, very small in terms of culture. But it was so striking, I mean you couldn't resist! The Greeks, as I said, the Greeks invented demonstration and politics simultaneously and we still have not worked out how to inherit the two inventions. But we should not mix them.

Edgar Whitley

Okay, Noortje, do you want to make a final comment? You don't have to.

Noorjte Marres

No, no, not necessarily.

Edgar Whitley

Okay, Graham?

Graham Harman

Yes. [LAUGHTER] I just wanted to say thanks again to the ANTHEM people. And one of the things that Peter and I have been joking about, somewhat to my horror, is that this event almost proves Bruno's theories and disproves mine, because none of the actors involved were very strong by themselves. It took many different people, and the manuscript itself, and many different organizers in the room, and all sorts of different agents to come together and make this event a reality. And so I want to thank everybody who was part of that. It has been an amazing experience to watch this event develop over the past four or five months. A series of incredible coincidences had to occur for this event even to occur, and I'm very happy that it happened as it did, and that all of you came.

Edgar Whitley

Just to sum up, I was scribbling various notes just on some of the metaphors and images that I picked up... So we have had the industrial model of truth, we have had vicarious occasionalism.

Bruno has admitted he is an old-fashioned positivist, he is also a Darwinist, he doesn't have all of the answers, and irreduction is one of at least fourteen potential modes of existence. We have had discussions about Joliot's eyeballs and eardrums. We have had concern about serial re-describers but (careful) not serial killers, and we have had a little bit of discussion about art thieves. And I think towards the end of the discussion Bruno made a nice point that the common enemy, the common question that we have been addressing has been this idea of the information double-click, the transport without transformation. And the question has always been about keeping open the questions and not pre-assuming any of the things that we wanted to be looking into because that leads to academic poverty. And I think very much both Bruno's work over the years and Graham's book that is trying to tighten up and explore some of those things has been a very useful step in keeping open many of these questions, though it is all too easy to take short cuts to and to close those down.

So first of all, thanks very much to the audience: we have sociologists, business academics, media academics, architects, English scholars, geographers, philosophers and accountants and IS people, so a wonderful heterogeneous group of people here. Thanks to the IS Group for its support, both for arranging the event and also for lunch, etc. Thanks to Peter, Wifak, Ofer, Aleksi, Maha and others for doing all the setting up, for tidying up this room, making everything work, Fran back in the office, Noortje and Lucas for contributing to the panel and getting some of the discussions going, and of course to Bruno and Graham for their contributions. So thank you all very, very much.

[APPLAUSE]

Symposium Schedule

The Harman Review: Bruno Latour's Empirical Metaphysics

Hosted by the Information Systems and Innovation Group
Department of Management, London School of Economics and
Political Science

9:30-15:00
Tuesday, February 5, 2008
Graham Wallas Room
Old Building
Houghton Street
London School of Economics and Political Science

Schedule:

Time	Duration	Event
9:30-9:50	20 mins.	Registration (tea and coffee)
9:50-10:00	10 mins.	Welcome by Leslie Willcocks, Head of ISIG, LSE
10:00-10:10	10 mins.	Chair's Introduction - Edgar Whitley
10:10-10:40	30 mins.	Graham Harman's presentation
10:40-11:20	40 mins.	Bruno Latour's response

11:20-11:30	10 mins.	Graham Harman's response to Bruno Latour's response
11:30-12:00	30 mins.	Audience questions, comments, and discussion
12:00-12:45	45 mins.	Lunch
12:45-13:30	45 mins.	Panel Discussion with Bruno Latour, Graham Harman, Lucas Introna, and Noortje Marres, chaired by Edgar Whitley
13:30-13:45	15 mins.	Graham Harman's closing statement
13:45-14:00	15 minutes	Bruno Latour's closing statement
14:00-14:10	10 minutes	Chair's closing statement - Edgar Whitley
14:10-15:00	50 minutes	Tea and coffee, informal chat and farewells

About the speakers, the panel and the chair:

Bruno Latour is Professor and Vice-President for Research at Sciences-Po Paris

Graham Harman is Associate Professor of Philosophy at the American University in Cairo and currently Visiting Associate Professor of Metaphysics and the Philosophy of Science at the University of Amsterdam

Lucas Introna is Professor of Organisation, Technology and Ethics and Head of the Department of Organisation, Work and Technology at Lancaster University Management School

Noortje Marres is Marie Curie Research Fellow at the Centre for the Study of Invention and Social Process, Department of Sociology, Goldsmiths, University of London

Edgar Whitley is Reader in the Information Systems and Innovation Group, Department of Management, London School of Economics and Political Science

This symposium has been organized by members of the ANTHEM Group:

http://www.anthem-group.net

Symposium Organizing Committee:

Aleksi Aaltonen, PhD Candidate, ISIG, LSE
Ofer Engel, PhD Candidate, ISIG, LSE
Peter Erdélyi, PhD Candidate, ISIG, LSE
Wifak Houij Gueddana, PhD Candidate, ISIG, LSE
Dr Maha Shaikh, Research Officer, ISIG, LSE

Participants' Questions and Comments

NOTE: All participants were offered the opportunity to submit a question or a comment by email to the panel in advance, in order to provide material for the afternoon panel discussion. Submissions are listed below in the order in which they were received.

Michael Witmore

In the middle of Shakespeare's *King Lear*, the fool asks the old king "the reason why the seven stars are no more than seven?" to which Lear answers, "because they are not eight." Lear's answer is wonderful (the fool loves it) because it avoids appealing to what Harman calls the hidden depths of things and opts instead for a statement of what is actually the case, with the understanding that the actual is reason enough for its own being. While reading Harman's analysis of Latour's system, I felt sometimes that the power of the actual was so great that theoretical insight and present-tense description had become identical, as they do in Lear's answer. Is this a fair way of characterizing Harman's objection to Latour's "actualism": that it fails to explain something crucial by offering a description where really only a metaphysics will do? Is this a metaphysical objection (a critique of some lapse in logic) or is there a practical thrust to Harman's objection as well? For example, is there a still unformulated metaphysics of contact among mediators that would allow us to identify new types of black boxes in the world that would otherwise go unnoticed?

Aleksi Aaltonen

Could metaphysical and methodological readings of ANT live side-by-side?

The question of where the microbes were before Pasteur typically causes a heated debate whenever discussing Latour. And so it happened in our ANTHEM reading group. Harman provides the answer. Microbes did not exist before Pasteur made them exist, because everything that exists in the Latourian conception is understood as an event resulting from its associations.

Harman's argument is that denying any existence to entities before they are associated is a flaw in Latour's philosophy, but a flaw that can be remedied by being made more consistent in its fundamental principles. Harman makes, however, an interesting distinction between philosophical and empirical thinking: "An object can only be measured or registered by its relations, not fully defined by them. Pragmatism has value as a method, but it fails as a metaphysical doctrine."

Could there be both methodological *and* metaphysical readings of this controversy? To me the reading that Harman claims to be a mistake has been a quite insightful methodological tool.

Simon Mills

Harman writes: "To shift the scene of philosophy away from specific things is a superfluous gesture, and makes sense only if we lose faith in the concreteness of actors. Mammals are real, and *there is no good reason* to hold that mammals inhabit a topology that structures a space of possible vertebrates, as the wonderful Manuel DeLanda holds."

I would like to ask some questions related to the notion of individuation. Harman seems to be arguing here for a reality already comprised of fully constituted objects/actors. What account is there for how these objects are individuated: that is, how does this reality come to be constituted? If the world is "objects all the way down" then doesn't this open him up to accusations of atomism or hylemorphism, both of which are well-critiqued by Gilbert Simondon?

Although in the above quote Harman argues that there is "no good reason to hold that mammals inhabit a topology that structures a space of possible vertebrates" can he give an object-orientated account that is more reasonable?

Kellie Robertson

Since every new philosophy needs an acronym, it is clear that an "object-oriented philosophy of science" should, necessarily, be called OOPS. So within the domain of OOPS....

The treatise does an excellent job of bringing together classical philosophy (particularly Aristotle) with Latour (and, in passing, Descartes, Kant, Whitehead, Heidegger, Derrida, et alia) to illuminate the long-range philosophical stakes of an object-oriented philosophy. This contextualization is perhaps one of the book's greatest (among many great) strengths. Among the individual chapters, Graham's identification of *We Have Never Been Modern* as Latour's most provocative and ultimately most suggestive work seems right on the mark, and, consequently, this chapter seems to be the most important in the manuscript.

Graham provides an excellent summary of *We Have Never Been Modern*, obsessed as it is with the dance between Enlightenment strategies of purification and the ubiquitous hybrid objects that constantly undermine their claims. His identification of Latour as "nonmodern" is plausibly witty but also raises the question of what the relation is between the nonmodernist stance and that vast (and in Latour's book) essentially silent world of the so-called "premodern"? In questioning the false binary of nature and culture that Latour identifies as having arisen in the seventeenth century, Latour implicitly suggests that everything prior to the seventeenth century was a happy blur of person and thing, subject and object, living together in an undifferentiated utopia. I exaggerate, but there is a whiff of "paradise lost" in *We Have Never Been Modern* that has always made me uncomfortable. In this sense, Latour has become yet another victim of the modernity trope insofar as his debunking always and only comes from its own perspective. So my question for Graham is a rather specific (and self-serving medievalist-y) one:

In thinking about how an object-oriented philosophy destroys the foundational myths of modernity, what does it do for "pre-modernity"? If Latour argues that the seventeenth century began to misperceive a false distinction between people and things, is this just another version of Marx arguing that this misprision occurs with the inception of commodity relations and its subsequent fetishism? Aren't Latour and Marx essentially running parallel shell games just drawing different lines in the sand on the question of modernity? And, finally, how does your revision of Latour in the final chapter address such an admittedly unfashionable and historicist concern?

Wifak Houij Gueddana

Realism according to Latour is an 'acquirable' feature that is much depending on the extent to which a technical assemblage gains communality during a period of time. Then how does Latour understand time? According to Harman, "Latour holds that time is in fact produced by the labor of actors, which create an asymmetry of before and after." Both the concept of time and the notion of 'actor' combine to reveal an unresolved "tension" between events and trajectories. In this regard, what's the difference between a trajectory and an event from a methodological perspective? Is a researcher able to set boundaries between two or more actors, especially when they are in the process of 'transforming'?

Paolo Quattrone

It is difficult to ask one simple and clear question after reading a book that eloquently illustrates the huge breadth of Latour's work. I'll try below, by sticking to very general issues.

In what sense and to what extent can the principle of symmetry, for which human and non-humans are on the same footage, really free Latour from the difference between observer and observed, from the assumption that objects are out there for someone to be seen?

Although this point may not be Bruno's direct concern, the issue may have an impact (from an ontological point of view) on some key tenets of his philosophy.

The notion of translation, which is crucial to ANT, may also be subject to the same kind of criticism: Does the idea of translation really provide a new ontology? Something has to be translated into something else and it is thus still there. So change (still) happens in a linear spatio-temporal framework. This may be more flat than before (see Latour's *Reassembling the Social*) but it is still two-dimensional and ready to house objects of all sorts.

This ontological issue can also embrace other key ANT principles, such as, for example, the notion of action-at-a-distance and the creation of centers of calculation. These require a recursive process of accumulation of traces collected from the more dispersed peripheries. A process which happens in, and theoretically also requires, a linear spatio-temporal framework.

More recent work on Tarde seeks to move away from this impasse and I wonder how the "standard" ANT approach (of translations, obligatory passage points, action at a distance and centers of calculations) is combinable with Tarde's reverse reductionism and the like. Maybe the move from the verb 'to be' (which smells of ontology) to the verb 'to have' (which attracts and generates diversity) helps solving this theoretical conundrum.

Tom Eyers

I'd be interested to know what the panel makes of the "stubbornness" of things, their withdrawal, as a potential condition for agency. Further, has this not been neglected by the emphasis on relationality in ANT, as Harman has argued? Might we consider all objects "partial objects" to the extent that they withhold as much as they proffer, and in that sense what use might a selective and critical reading of psychoanalysis offer us? (Especially Lacan with the "objet a," etc.)

Nikiforos Panourgias

Does the notion of "explication" or "explicitation" that has received some mention from Latour himself (as well as in some other ANT circles) and that appears to suggest that different "folds" or aspects of reality are rendered explicit (or in a more concrete form) out of the trials that result from collisions of more durable/stable actor-networks with one another go some way toward answering the questions regarding potentiality that Harman raises? Which of the two names should be preferred, "explication" or "explicitation", is this something that is likely to be developed further, and if so, could we hear more about it?

Law and Mol move away from deploying the concept of a network in terms of describing the relations that constitute objects and instead prefer comparisons with fluids and the variable/flexible geometry of relations that the "fluid" metaphor favors. Is this part of the official program for the "recall" for repair of ANT?

Does Harman have a position about what travels/moves between actants? Does this have implications for his thesis and, if so, what might these be?

Alberto Toscano

Does the endeavor to avoid "modernist" practices of abstraction, separation and reductionism for the sake of a neo-monadological theory of actants not undermine any attempt to speculate about "the structure of reality"? In other words, can any metaphysics survive its demotion to just another "test of force," without being transformed into a merely ornamental or cynical activity, one far poorer in connections, alliances and *tests* than many any other activities one can think of? Isn't its subtraction from the domain of alliances constitutive of the very idea of a metaphysics or an ontology, at least as proposed by Harman?

Is there not something wholly arbitrary, or worse surreptitiously normative, about defining a non-reductive ontology or object-theory as "democratic"? Given the inspiration taken by Latour in theories of force and relation which were to say the least skeptical about liberal or socialist forms of democracy (Nietzsche, Tarde), what are we to make of the metapolitical invocations of "things set free" or a "parliament of things," alongside the suggestion that such a freeing of things is not unrelated to a freeing of persons?

Doesn't the more-or-less panpsychist dramatization of the alliances of actants in jauntily anthropomorphic terms enact the ultimate reduction, whereby objects and things are thought as analogies of human action, in ways far less challenging or surprising than the "reductive" explanations of mechanists and determinists?

Isabelle Doucet

I would be interested in addressing the association Graham Harman makes between the "medium in which translations occur... the medium for direct contact," and Latour's notion of "plasma" or "missing masses." According to Latour, "plasma" is what the network (or *worknets*) leaves unconnected... an outside about which we know not much. The plasma is the background, the not yet formatted... it is not hidden but simply unknown. I therefore did not see the plasma as the *medium* of relations, but as the not yet assembled, while at the same time being (possibly) real: even if unknown, it might affect something else. I believed it *could not* be a medium because if it *were*, it would unavoidably take part in the work of translation, and hence be involved in the assemblage, and connected. As a consequence it would no longer be plasma. But then Harman states that the plasma "might be formatted by other means than those of alliance." Then what precisely are those means and what are the implications for the real-ness of the plasma (to resist or give way)? And how does this link up with Harman's view on the plasma as lying "on the interior of objects themselves"?

Notes

1. Harman, G. (2009). *Prince of Networks: Bruno Latour and Metaphysics*. Melbourne, re.press.
2. Ibid. p. 5.
3. Willcocks, L. and E. Whitley (2009). "Developing the Information and Knowledge Agenda in Information Systems: Insights From Philosophy." *The Information Society* 25: 190-197.
4. The LSE's Department of Information Systems later became the Information Systems and Innovation Group (ISIG) in the newly formed Department of Management.
5. Heidegger, M. (1977). *The Question Concerning Technology and Other Essays*. New York; London, Harper and Row.
6. Latour, B. (2007). "Can We Get Our Materialism Back, Please?" *Isis* 98: 138–142.
7. C.f. Ciborra, C. U. and O. Hanseth (1998). "From Tool to Gestell: Agendas for Managing the Information Infrastructure " *Information Technology & People* 11(4): 305-327 and Whitley, E.A. (1998) Understanding Participation in Entrepreneurial Organizations: Applying the Sociology of Translation. In *Sixth European Conference on Information Systems*, Baets, W. (ed.) (Euro-Arab Management School, Aix-en-Provence, France), pp. 1225-37, a revised and extended version of which was later published as Whitley, E. A. (1999). "Understanding Participation in Entrepreneurial Organizations: Some Hermeneutic Readings." *Journal of Information Technology* 14: 193-202.
8. See e.g. Introna, L. (2007). "Maintaining the Reversibility of Foldings: Making the Ethics (Politics) of Information Technology Visible." *Ethics and Information Technology* 9(1): 11-25. and Introna, L. D. (2009). "Ethics and the Speaking of Things." *Theory Culture Society* 26(4): 25-46.
9. Latour, B. (2004). "On Using ANT for Studying Information Systems: A (Somewhat) Socratic Dialogue." *The Social Study of*

Information and Communication Technology: Innovation, Actors and Contexts. Ed. by C. Avgerou, C. Ciborra and F. Land. Oxford, Oxford University Press: 62-76. Also published as a chapter in Latour, B. (2005). *Reassembling the Social: An Introduction to Actor-Network-Theory.* Oxford; New York, Oxford University Press.

10. For a selected bibliography, see the ANTHEM blog: http://anthem-group.net/bibliography/

11. This paper has been published as Chapter 5 in Harman, G. (2010). *Towards Speculative Realism: Essays and Lectures.* Winchester, UK: zerO Books.

12. For Latour's use of Heidegger's concepts, see e.g. Latour, B. (2005). "From Realpolitik to Dingpolitik or How to Make Things Public." *Making Things Public: Atmospheres of Democracy.* Ed. by B. Latour and P. Weibel. Cambridge, Mass.; London, MIT: 14-41. or Latour, B. (2004). "Why Has Critique Run Out of Steam? From Matters of Fact to Matters of Concern." *Critical Inquiry* 30(2): 225-248.

13. PowerPoint slides and a recording of the talk are available on the LSE website: http://www.lse.ac.uk/collections/information Systems/newsAndEvents/2007events/harman.htm

14. Exercices de métaphysique empirique (autour des travaux de Bruno Latour), June 23-30, 2007, Cerisy-la-Salle, France: http://www.ccic-cerisy.asso.fr/latour07.html

15. Bruno Latour and Barbara Vanderlinden, "Park Nights: Laboratorium," Serpentine Gallery, Hyde Park, London.

16. Heidegger, M. (1993). "What is Metaphysics?" *Basic Writings: from Being and Time (1927) to The Task of Thinking (1964).* New York, Harper San Francisco: 89-110.

17. Latour, B. (2005). *Reassembling the Social: An Introduction to Actor-Network-Theory.* Oxford; New York, Oxford University Press. p. 72.

18. Heidegger, M. (1975). "The Thing." *Poetry, Language, Thought.* New York, Harper & Row: p. 172.

19. Latour, B. (2005). "From Realpolitik to Dingpolitik or How to Make Things Public." Op. cit. See also the articles in Chapter 4, "From Objects to Things" (pp. 250-295), in the same volume.
20. In chronological order, these talks were as follows: "The Origin of the Work of Art (atonal remix)" at the Arts Institute at Bournemouth, February 1, 2008; "The Greatness of McLuhan" at the Media School, Bournemouth University, February 4, 2008; "Actor-Network Metaphysics" at Lancaster University Management School, February 6, 2008; "The Causal Medium: McLuhan's Fourfold Space" at the Department of Geography, Open University, Milton Keynes, February 7, 2008; and "Weird Ontology" at the University of the West of England, Bristol, February 13, 2008.
21. A recording of Latour's lecture is available from the LSE website: http://richmedia.lse.ac.uk/publicLecturesAndEvents /20080204_1830_anotherEuropeanTraditionTraceabilityOfThe SocialAndTheVindicationOfGabrielTarde.mp3
22. Recordings are available for Harman's two talks in Bournemouth: "On the Origin of the Work of Art (atonal remix)" at the Arts Institute at Bournemouth on February 1, 2008: http://anthem-group.net/2008/02/08/recording-of-graham-harmans-talk-at-aib/ and "The Greatness of McLuhan" at the Media School, Bournemouth University on February 4, 2008: http://anthem-group.net/2008/02/08/recording-of-graham-harmans-talk-at-the-media-school-at-bournemouth-university/
23. The fire alarm incident has nonetheless left a trace in the blogosphere: http://testsociety.wordpress.com/2008/02/13/more-realism/
24. See Latour, B. (1999). "On Recalling ANT." *Actor Network Theory and After*. Eds. J. Law and J. Hassard. Oxford, Blackwell's for Sociological Review: 15-25.
25. URLs for the Harman Review recording on the LSE website and the ANTHEM blog: http://www.lse.ac.uk/collections

/informationSystems/newsAndEvents/2008events/HarmanLat
our.htm
http://anthem-group.net/2008/02/08/recording-of-the-harman-
review-bruno-latours-empirical-metaphysics/
26. Latour, B. and S. Woolgar (1986). *Laboratory Life: The Construction of Scientific Facts*. Princeton, N.J, Princeton University Press. p. 88.
27. Ibid. p. 51.
28. Avgerou, C., Ciborra, C., Land F. (eds.) (2003) *The Social Study of Information and Communication Technologies*. Oxford University Press, Oxford
29. Mingers, J. and Willcocks, L. (2003) *Social Theory and Philosophy For Information Systems*, Wiley Chichester
30. Bruno Latour's lecture at the LSE on February 4, 2008, entitled "Another European Tradition: traceability of the social and the vindication of Gabriel Tarde."
31. "Bruno Latour, King of Networks," lecture delivered by Harman on April 16, 1999 at the Department of Philosophy at DePaul University, Chicago. Published in Graham Harman, *Towards Speculative Realism: Essays and Lectures*. (Winchester, UK: Zero Books, 2010.) Pages 67-92.
32. Latour, B. (1988). *The Pasteurization of France*. Cambridge, Mass.: Harvard University Press.
33. Latour, B. (1999). *Pandora's Hope: Essays on the Reality of Science Studies*. Cambridge, Mass.: Harvard University Press.
34. Meillassoux, Q. (2008). *Après la finitude: An Essay on the Necessity of Contingency*. London: Continuum.
35. Latour, B. (1996) *Aramis, or the Love of Technology*. Cambridge, Mass., Harvard University Press.
36. Latour, B. (2009). *The Making of Law: An Ethnography of the Conseil D'etat*, Polity Press.
37. Exercices de métaphysique empirique (autour des travaux de Bruno Latour), Centre Culturel International de Cerisy-La-Salle, France. June 24-29, 2007.

38. DeLanda, M. (2006). A *New Philosophy of Society: Assemblage Theory and Social Complexity*. London: Continuum.
39. Harman, G. (2007). *Heidegger Explained: From Phenomenon to Thing*. Chicago: Open Court.
40. Latour, B. (2008). "Review Essay: The Netz-Works of Greek Deductions." *Social Studies of Science* 38 (3): 441-459.
41. Netz, R. (2003), *The Shaping of Deduction in Greek Mathematics: A Study in Cognitive History*. Cambridge: Cambridge University Press
42. See Latour, B. and Lowe, A. (2011). "The migration of the aura, or how to explore the original through its facsimiles." In: Bartscherer, T. and Coover, R. (eds.), Switching Codes. Chicago: University of Chicago Press, available at http://WWW.bruno-latour.fr/articles/article/108-ADAM-FACSIMILES-AL-BL.pdf.
43. Marres, N. & Sonderegger R. (2007) Interview with Graham Harman (in Dutch), "De objectgerichte filosofie van Graham Harman", *KRISIS: Tijdschrift voor Actuele Filosofie* (4): 65-79.
44. Latour, B. (2007). "A Plea for Earthly Sciences." *Keynote Lecture for the annual meeting of the British Sociological Association*, from http://www.bruno-latour.fr/articles/article/102-BSA-GB.pdf.
45. Latour, B. (1999). *Pandora's Hope: Essays on the Reality of Science Studies*. Cambridge, Mass., London, Harvard University Press.
46. "On Actors, Networks, and Plasma: Heidegger vs. Latour vs. Heidegger." Information Systems Research Forum, Information Systems and Innovation Group, Department of Management, LSE, November 29, 2007 (audio recording available at: http://www.lse.ac.uk/collections/information Systems/newsAndEvents/2007events/harman.htm)
47. Deleuze, G. (1994). *Difference and Repetition*. London, Athlone.
48. Law, J. (1986). "On the Methods of Long Distance Control: Vessels, Navigation and the Portuguese Route to India." *Power, Action and Belief: A New Sociology of Knowledge? Sociological Review Monograph*. J. Law. London, Routledge and Kegan Paul.

32: 234-263.

49. Kupiec, J.-J. & Sonigo, P. (2000). *Ni Dieu ni gène. Pour une autre théorie de l'hérédité.* Seuil.

50. Bruno Latour's lecture at the LSE on February 4, 2008 entitled "Another European Tradition: traceability of the social and the vindication of Gabriel Tarde."

51. www.bruno-latour.fr/articles/article/104-NETZ-SSofS.pdf

Contemporary culture has eliminated both the concept of the public and the figure of the intellectual. Former public spaces – both physical and cultural – are now either derelict or colonized by advertising. A cretinous anti-intellectualism presides, cheerled by expensively educated hacks in the pay of multinational corporations who reassure their bored readers that there is no need to rouse themselves from their interpassive stupor. The informal censorship internalized and propagated by the cultural workers of late capitalism generates a banal conformity that the propaganda chiefs of Stalinism could only ever have dreamt of imposing. Zer0 Books knows that another kind of discourse – intellectual without being academic, popular without being populist – is not only possible: it is already flourishing, in the regions beyond the striplit malls of so-called mass media and the neurotically bureaucratic halls of the academy. Zer0 is committed to the idea of publishing as a making public of the intellectual. It is convinced that in the unthinking, blandly consensual culture in which we live, critical and engaged theoretical reflection is more important than ever before.